Elizabeth J Dennison

DRY TEARS

D0957661

DRY TEARS

The Story of a Lost Childhood

NECHAMA TEC

New York
OXFORD UNIVERSITY PRESS

OXFORD UNIVERSITY PRESS
Oxford   London   Glasgow
New York   Toronto   Melbourne   Wellington
Nairobi   Dar es Salaam   Cape Town
Kuala Lumpur   Singapore   Jakarta   Hong Kong   Tokyo
Delhi   Bombay   Calcutta   Madras   Karachi

Copyright © 1982, 1984 by Nechama Tec
First published in 1982 by Wildcat Publishing Company, Inc.,
Westport, Connecticut
First issued in paperback in 1984 by Oxford University
Press, Inc., 200 Madison Avenue, New York, NY 10016
Reprinted, with a new Epilogue, by arrangement with
Wildcat Publishing Company

Library of Congress Cataloging in Publication Data

Tec, Nechama.
Dry tears.

Reprint. Originally published: Westport, Conn.:
Wildcat Pub. Co., c1982. With new epilogue.
1. Holocaust, Jewish (1939–1945)—Personal
narratives. 2. Tec, Nechama. I. Title.
D810.J4T42   1984   940.53′15′03924   84-1069
ISBN 0-19-503500-3 (pbk.)

Printing (last digit):   9 8 7

Printed in the United States of America

To my mother, Estera Hachamoff,
and my late father, Roman Bawnik

Acknowledgments

The encouragement and strength to embark upon and complete the writing of this book came from several sources. Most vital was the steadfast approval and inspiration I received from my husband Leon and my children Leora and Roland. Without their total involvement and constant support this book would not have happened. I am grateful to my friend and publisher, Carol Plaine Fisher, for her confidence and trust and sensitive awareness of my inner struggles. And warm thanks to Selma Weitz for the enthusiasm and support which invariably accompanied her expert typing of this book.

For the opportunity to have *Dry Tears* republished, I wish to thank Susan Rabiner, my Oxford University Press editor. I am particularly grateful for Susan's patience, her gentle, yet firm prodding, that made my writing of the epilogue possible.

Contents

CHAPTER ONE

— ◆▶◆ —

The Approaching Shadow

Shortly after the occupation of Lublin in 1939 Jewish children had been barred from attending school and private instruction was prohibited. As with all such Nazi directives, disobedience if discovered met with severe punishment, even death.

When our own school was closed—I was eight at the time—I was not in the least upset. But my parents reacted differently. They insisted that after the war my sister and I would need all the education we could get. And although I could not share their love and respect for education, their conviction that for us there would be an "after the war" impressed me. Like them, I too believed that we would survive the war.

Before long my parents engaged Hela Trachtenberg, the daughter of my father's accountant, to tutor my sister and me. Thirty, single, eager to earn a living, Hela had recently come from Warsaw, where she had been working as a high school teacher. Highly educated and reliable, she was well suited for her new position. My parents arranged for her to come to our house at least four hours each day. She was to instruct us in all subjects, including Latin, mathematics, science, and literature.

1

My sister and I were at once curious and apprehensive about our teacher. Her age placed her automatically in the category of old maid, concerning whom we had strange ideas, none of them positive. Determined to learn more about Hela, we pestered our parents with questions. We learned only that in Warsaw she had been engaged to a lawyer who had abruptly walked out of her life. This vague report gave rise to many conjectures, none of which were important, and none of which we could verify. In any case, I was opposed to lessons of all sorts, and especially to lessons from someone who, I decided, by the nature of things, was sure to be an inferior teacher.

But no one consulted me, and the morning arrived when I met Hela Trachtenberg. As we shook hands I was stiff and ill at ease, fearful that I would inadvertently show my resentment. Hela gave me a penetrating look, followed by a broad smile. "She is trying to bribe me," I thought. Still distrustful, still curious, I noticed that the gray eyes behind her glasses, though squinting, were unusually lively and intelligent. Beginning to relax a little, I also noticed that Hela Trachtenberg was of medium height and slim, with ash-blond hair and regular features. Because of the squint and her pallor she was not attractive. And yet, right then and there, I did realize that she was special. There was something open about her. Without being able to put my feelings into words I sensed in her a certain strength, combined with gentleness and kindness, all enlivened by.wit. There was a charming twinkle in those eyes behind the glasses. I could not resist her. I felt all my reservations melting away. A glance at my sister told me that she too was strongly drawn to this stranger.

Then I heard a soft melodious voice. "I am Hela Trachtenberg. I've come to teach you. I hope it will be fun for all of us. Let me first find out what you know." She wanted us to take a test right then and there. And right then and there I said, "Miss Hela, I don't like to study. I wish I didn't have to learn anything." I expected her to be annoyed. Instead, the twinkle showed again, and then in a matter-of-fact way she said: "I will try to make it exciting for you. Maybe that will change your attitude."

From that moment on my relation to our new teacher was different from what I had expected it to be. Not only did she succeed in making learning exciting, but she also tried unobtrusively to teach me about basic decency, fairness, and compassion. She urged me never to lose my sense of humor: "Helka, remember, if you find nothing else funny in life, at least you can laugh at yourself. I pity those who cannot do that." True to her philosophy, she never took herself too seriously.

Soon my sister and I grew to love our Hela and called her "Czuczka," a term of endearment even though it meant piglet. At first it was my desire to please her that prompted me to study. But by degrees, working became a habit. Czuczka in turn had a marvelous way of applauding me for my efforts and disregarding my failures, and I was eager to earn her approval. Often I would think before I acted. How would Czuczka look at it? Would she do this, and would she do it the same way? Usually such decisions involved sharing a rare delicacy, keeping someone's secret, or deciding on how much help to give to whom. And even though most of the time I did not mention such problems to her, I knew she would urge me to be good, just, and decent. Invariably, thinking about her helped me make the right decision.

I wasn't the only one on whom Czuczka had this positive effect. My sister and my parents each in a different way became as attached to her as I was. Indeed, now that Czuczka had become so much a part of our life, everything began to look better, somehow less threatening.

In reality, of course, our situation remained as strange and precarious as ever. We were cramped into one small room, where simultaneously my sister was learning Latin, I was struggling with a composition, and all of us were listening—always listening— for danger signals from the hostile world around us. Any of us could be shot simply because I was trying to memorize a poem! And yet it never occurred to even one of us that my sister and I should give up studying.

Our secret education was only a small aspect of the strange and irrational nature our lives had taken on. In general, few things made sense to us. The Nazis seemed so unpredictable. Here and there they made exceptions to their policy of destruction, and this only intensified the widespread confusion, uncertainty, and fear.

One of the Nazis' strange exceptions was a group of Jewish soldiers who had been taken prisoner at the start of the German invasion. They were confined along with Russian soldiers in a special camp. All of them engaged in hard labor, they all lived in the most primitive conditions, and they were all treated with the customary Nazi cruelty. Surprisingly, however, the Russians received worse treatment than the Jews. Food, for instance, was distributed to the Russians in smaller amounts and was of poorer quality. The Russians in fact looked as if they might die of starvation at any minute, and rumor said their condition was so desperate that they fed on their dead comrades. The smallest transgression on their part, even an inability to work because of severe illness, met with death. They were a pitiful group, and their numbers were shrinking rapidly.

In contrast, besides being better fed the Jewish prisoners had more freedom than the Russians. They were given permission to visit the Jewish part of the city. Only a few of them took advantage of that privilege by attempting to escape. The terrible consequences of recapture and the threat of reprisals—for every man who escaped, ten of his comrades would be killed—no doubt weighed heavily against such an attempt. In any event, they were not so badly off as yet.

The local Jews took a special interest in them. They were attractive and seemingly carefree young men who were pleasant to have around; they became a much needed and welcome diversion. They appealed to the young women and, in the year or so in which they were allowed some freedom to come and go, many marriages were contracted.

We ourselves welcomed three or four of these prisoners and tried to make them feel a part of the family. On holidays, when they had more free time, they would come in the morning and stay as long as possible, eating, joking, and singing. Their visits added joy to our otherwise dreary existence. Perhaps inevitably, one of them fell in love with my sister who, though not yet fifteen, was mature, intelligent, and very pretty. I had no trouble understanding her appeal for him. But in view of her youth, and the fact that men younger and more attractive than he were available, I didn't understand his appeal for her. Not only was he "old," about thirty-three, but he was bald and rather short, and he had a limp. As I came to know him better, I had to admit that his pleasant personality compensated for his age and appearance. He was intelligent and thoughtful, and fond of discussing what to me were incomprehensible topics.

When it became obvious that he and my sister were serious about each other, my parents, who had been disturbed by the relationship from the start, made it clear that he was unwelcome in our house. But he and my sister were not easily defeated. They decided to see each other in secret. Their meetings took place on deserted streets, and I went along as an unofficial chaperon. Winter had come, and such meetings were not without price. The three of us would meet and start walking. I stayed in front, they followed a few steps behind. I never looked back, although I made a great effort to hear what they were saying. As far as I could tell, their conversations were on a high intellectual plane. These very innocent meetings remained limited to talking. Still, my being a part of the relationship made me feel grown up and special.

The relative freedom allowed these Jewish prisoners was one of those capricious Nazi gestures so common during the occupation. Of course the leniency did not last. Eventually the Nazis would subject the prisoners to the same treatment as all other Jews. But at that time, few of us knew or wanted to know what was in store. My father was one of those who did.

"Work," my father explained, "is now a matter of life and death." Almost immediately after the Germans invaded Poland it had become dangerous to be without work. The papers my father had received when the Germans took over our chemical factory were about to expire and he felt they would not be renewed unless he actually worked in the factory. He went to see the German commissioner who was in charge there, to ask for a job that would provide proper identification.

The commissioner received him icily: "The other Jewish factory owners started working immediately," he said. "They deserve the papers. Now all the positions are filled. You, Mr. Bawnik, are too late. I can do nothing for you."

Without a word my father stood up and moved toward the door. "Wait," the German said. "Aren't you going to ask me to reconsider? Have you nothing at all to say?"

"If you can't even offer me a job and the papers to go with it after all the years of hard work I have put into this place," my father answered, "there is nothing left to say."

Silence followed. Then the commissioner invited my father to sit down. "I like your courage," he told him. "I believe I can find a place for you and I will give you good papers. You are a chemist. You will be listed as indispensable."

My father was only a self-taught chemist. Chemistry was his hobby, not his profession, as the German knew; but he chose to overlook it.

Even though after that my father's papers protected the whole family, my mother preferred to work, also. She found a job as a housekeeper for a high Nazi official, and became what the Nazis considered a useful Jew in her own right.

Besides adding safety, my mother's work had other advantages. Except for bread, food was becoming scarce. It was harder and harder to find meat, eggs, sugar, and milk. My mother was an excellent housekeeper, conscientious and hard working, and her employers liked her enough to reward her with baskets of food.

Of course the meat that was a part of these gifts was not kosher. But my mother, who until then had kept a kosher home and had refused to taste any of the forbidden foods, stopped objecting. Appalled by the destruction around her, she had concluded simply: "There is no God. If there were a God he could not tolerate all the murdering and torturing of innocent people." Just as she previously had had. no doubts about observing religious rituals, now she did not hesitate to give them up. Those few simple words were all the justification she needed. She was a person of action, not given to brooding.

The change was made easier for her because my Orthodox grandparents were far away in their little town. We still got mail from them, and my mother went out of her way to supply them with money and goods. But Jews were not allowed to travel and visits were out of the question. So my grandparents never knew that the daughter who was so docile and submissive to them, the one who helped them most, had rejected religion.

Mother's job also provided her with useful information. Her employer knew a great deal. As she served meals she learned from conversations at the table that what the Germans called "deportations" were often executions—that groups of Jews who were rounded up in raids were taken no farther than a nearby forest, where they were shot.

My mother passed on the stories, but people did not believe her. They felt she must be exaggerating—that she was one of those people who can only see the dark side of life. Still she felt compelled to share her knowledge, and despite the scorn she continued to report all the news that came her way.

Only my father encouraged her. "Find out all you can," he urged her. "Ignorance is dangerous." He was less emotional and less dramatic than my mother, and he did not press his views on others. When he voiced an opinion he did it in an understated and unhurried way, and perhaps for that very reason people listened to him more than to my mother.

Although neither of my parents had any illusions about the dangers that lay ahead, they steadfastly believed in our ultimate survival. It was this trust in a better future, coupled with an awareness of the seriousness of our situation, that they tried to impress upon my sister and me. Without sparing us the details of Nazi atrocities, they kept repeating, "If you are going to survive, you must use your wits and you must know what it is all about. You must grow up fast." Part of this growing up was knowing about money, which my parents increasingly felt would be a key to our survival. They continued to convert money into jewelry, gold, and American dollars, which were then sewn into our clothes. Each of us also wore a small cloth bag filled with valuables around our necks, hidden under our clothing.

As we were trying to learn how to stay alive the destruction around us continued. The sick, the disabled, and the "unproductive" Jews became special targets. In the middle of the night the SS would descend on Jewish hospitals and kill each patient who was too weak to walk. Many of those who could walk were loaded into trucks and taken away, never to be heard from again. The remainder, usually only a handful, were allowed to stay on.

A similar fate was reserved for children in orphanages, who were also being ordered from their beds in late-night raids. Those who hesitated, the SS killed on the spot. The rest were moved into the courtyards where they were told to form orderly lines and shot systematically, one by one.

When there were no more Jewish orphanages, and when most of the hospital patients had perished, the Nazis turned to the rest of the Jewish population. They would surround a Jewish building in the middle of the night, order all Jews into the courtyard, and divide them into "the more and the less useful." Usually those who looked a little weaker or older, often women with children, were put in the "useless" group and taken away, vanishing forever from sight.

My Aunt Ella, her husband, and their three children disappeared during one such raid. For many days my father made inquiries whenever and wherever he could. His efforts uncovered nothing but conflicting rumors. We heard that they had been deported for heavy labor to the East; that they had been sent to a concentration camp; that they had been shot on the outskirts of Lublin. When my father finally gave up searching he became unusually quiet. To our questions he simply answered, "We shall not see them again." The expression on his face, at once full of pain and resigned, told us that he would not elaborate. He mourned privately. Not to hurt him, we stayed away from the subject. We never saw my Aunt Ella and her family again, and we never knew how they perished.

In another raid my easygoing Uncle Josef, my mother's brother, lost his wife and their two sons. He was spared because the work he was doing was useful to the Germans. Shaken by his loss, he behaved as if part of him had died. He started visiting us more often than before. No matter how welcome we made him, we could not help him recapture his old lust for life. The careless, fun-loving part of his personality had vanished forever.

People continued to disappear. By now we rarely asked questions and had little time to mourn. We smiled less, felt growing fear, and waited. We saw the changes but they came too fast and we could not adjust to them, could not grasp that they were actual or believe that they were permanent.

Each time a new purge took place and the number of Jews shrank further, we preferred to think of it as the last blow, and told ourselves that the rest of us would be spared. The Germans fostered such beliefs by issuing proclamations after each action—or *Aktion*, as they called it—to assure the remaining Jews that they would continue to live peacefully in the manner to which they were accustomed. And life did go on.

And then one evening my mother came home from her work in a state of terrible agitation. "We are lost, we are lost," was all she could say. When she finally calmed down, we learned that the German official's wife had told her that from now on she would not be able to employ her. The German wept as she explained why. "Tonight," the German said, "all Jews will be awakened late at night. The majority will be deported, the rest will be moved to a special area evacuated by Poles on the outskirts of Lublin. From now on no Jew will be allowed to work for a private family. How will I manage this household without you? How?" As an afterthought, she added,

"Believe me, deportation is bad. Save yourself." Now as before our neighbors with whom mother tried to share this information refused to believe her, and felt she was exaggerating.

It was late, and we had to act swiftly. Much of the brief discussion between my parents I did not understand. There was no time for explanations. We collected our most valuable belongings, left the rest behind, and walked quickly to the chemical factory.

The German commissioner received us with courtesy and kindness. He listened to what my father said and asked no questions. He was eager to help. "I will do all I can to protect you," he said. "You are not to worry. You will work here and I will legalize your stay. From now on this will be your home."

He took us into an unused part of the factory, a huge room located one flight above the ground. It must have been at least one hundred fifty feet long and thirty feet wide, with twenty or so windows all facing the street. The size and bareness of the place seemed eerie, and I moved closer to my mother. Then I saw my father reach into his pocket and hand the commissioner a small bag that I knew contained gold and valuable jewelry. As he did so he said: "I hope that you will agree to keep this for all and any of us. It will be safer with you than with me."

The German looked surprised and pleased. "I will guard it well, and return it at any time of your choosing," he told my father.

Even though I knew that this commissioner was very different from every other Nazi I had seen or heard about, I was surprised by all that was happening. Was my father right in trusting this man? It was a nagging question that came into my mind again and again. But of course I said nothing.

That same evening the Polish janitor helped us move into our new quarters. Beds, a wardrobe, a small stove, and two crates to serve as chairs were placed in a corner of the room. The transition from our cramped home had been sudden. None of us said much. None of us slept well. I kept tossing, turning, hoping that no action against the Jews would take place and that when tomorrow came we would leave this vast, empty, unfriendly room.

Unfortunately, however, what my mother's employer had told her proved to be correct. In the morning we were joined by one of my father's partners, who brought the first account of the devastating purge. During the night scores of SS had descended upon the entire Jewish population, which by then was concentrated in a small section of town. All were ordered out of their apartments and into the courtyards. In accordance with the established practice, those who were ill or were for any reason too weak to move were murdered on the spot. The rest were divided into two groups. Papers helped little and pleas from families that they be allowed to stay together had no effect. During the sorting out, many persons—men, women, and children alike— were severely beaten, and those who fell to the ground were shot.

Of the two groups, the larger one was made up of the wounded who had managed to stay upright, women with children, older men, and women, and a few young men. They were destined for deportation, no one knew where. The second group consisted of healthy-looking individuals, more of them men than women, and very few of them children. This group was moved to the new ghetto, a worker's settlement called Majdan Tatarski.

When more detailed news began to reach us, we heard that Czuczka and her family had been transferred to the ghetto. We also learned that among those who had vanished were two families with whom we had shared our cramped apartment. Ironically, they had been the most skeptical about the alarming reports my mother had brought from her German employers. More shattering to us was the news about my mother's brother, Josef. He too had disappeared. Rumors began to circulate about what had become of him. Some were wild, some strange but plausible enough to be frightening. We found all the rumors hard to believe. My mother often wept, but refused to think that Josef was gone forever.

Then, early one evening, less than a week after learning of his disappearance, we were sitting in our corner of the huge room when we heard someone hesitantly come to the door. We watched it swing open and saw a tall man, unshaven, dressed in dirty, torn clothes. Badly bent over, he gave the impression of someone who had shrunk completely into himself. Fearfully and tentatively he looked around. I heard my mother scream: "Josef, oh my God, it is my Josef!" She threw herself upon him, sobbing uncontrollably. The rest of us surrounded him, hugging, kissing, laughing and crying. Josef stood there smiling faintly, as if embarrassed, looking thin and tired. Then little by little he told us what had happened. On the night of deportation together with many others he was packed closely into a freight car. None of them knew where they were being taken. Because of the terrible crowding, the lack of air, food, and water, many people died. Growing numbers of dead bodies began to fill the car. Josef was convinced that he would soon become one of them.

He explained that he had jumped off the moving train not so much to save himself, but to die breathing fresh air. Two other men jumped with him. All three landed in a ditch. One of them was shot and died on the spot; the other was seriously wounded. The guards kept shooting. Josef stayed in the ditch, pretending to be dead. Only much later, long after the shooting stopped, did he crawl out, leaving behind him both the dead and the wounded man.

Once out of the ditch, Josef moved cautiously. Determined to stay away from people, he hid whenever he heard voices or steps. He ate whatever he could find in the fields. Walking at night, hiding for most of the day, he lost all sense of time.

When Josef finished his story he looked through us rather than at us. Then, talking as if to himself, he shook his head in disbelief. "I never thought that I would make it. I never thought, never . . ." Strangely, he behaved as if in fact he had not made it. He did not share in our excitement and happiness. But my mother was oblivious to his mood. Whenever her eyes rested on him they assumed a special glow. She was happier than I had seen her in a long time.

The Commissioner agreed to employ Josef and said that he might stay with us. Everything seemed to be moving along smoothly. Then, after my uncle's second work day, the janitor's wife burst into our room, whispering loudly: "Run, run. The Gestapo is here. They are looking for Josef." Just as fast as she had come she disappeared. Then we heard the heavy tread of boots coming up the stairs. Without a word my father pushed Josef into the wardrobe and quickly rearranged the clothes inside to hide him. The wardrobe door remained open, but Josef had become invisible. The janitor, pale and shaky, came into the room, followed by two Gestapo officers. I was afraid to look at them, afraid to meet their eyes. I kept my own eyes on their highly polished boots.

One of the officers turned to my mother: "Your brother is here. There is no point in denying it—we have complete information. Where is he?" Then he turned to my father: "Your papers."

The janitor opened his mouth to say something, probably to help us, but he shut it again without a sound. The officer examined my father's papers and returned them without comment.

"I have not seen my brother in a long time," I heard my mother say. The response to her words was a heavy blow, which landed somewhere between her head and shoulder. She staggered but made no sound. The officers signaled to each other and began their search. They looked under each bed, in the corners, behind the wardrobe. They passed the open door of the wardrobe without bothering to look inside. My heart was beating fast and loud and I was almost choking. I was afraid to move, afraid to breathe, and especially afraid to change my expression. Soon they were through searching and were mumbling angrily under their breath. I heard one of them say: "We are taking you instead. It is either you or your brother."

Without a word my mother moved toward them. I felt dizzy. Nausea overcame me as I watched her walk toward the door, an officer on each side. No one made a sound. The silence was complete, deadly. Then I heard my father's voice loud and clear: "He is here. Take him. She is a mother." He pointed toward the wardrobe.

Swiftly the Germans reached for Josef, and without giving him a chance to move, they kicked him as they dragged him along. All this happened very fast. Too fast. They disappeared outside beyond the door. My mother—helplessly crying, "Josef, Josef, Josef . . ."—tried to follow. But father caught her by the shoulder and held her firmly against him. She struggled to break free. Sobbing with pain, she kept repeating, "Roman, why did you do it, why, Roman, why?"

With great difficulty the three of us put her to bed. Nothing soothed her. She fluctuated between fits of crying and bitter accusations against my father. Only twice did I hear him say softly: "It was not right. He should have come out on his own. The children need a mother." He remained calm and did not otherwise disagree with her. He applied a cold wet rag to her forehead and red eyes. My mother refused his help and angrily kept pushing him away. At dawn, exhausted, she fell asleep.

In the morning, when she refused to dress, my father insisted that she get ready for work. "I will spare no effort to get Josef back if you go about your duties. You must live," he said. Slowly my mother did get dressed, and went to work without breakfast.

For some days afterward she moved automatically through the daily routine, taking no interest either in us or in what she was doing. At times I heard her whisper to herself: "I should have saved him. It is all my fault."

True to his promise my father set about rescuing Josef. First he had to locate him. At that time people felt a strong obligation to provide each other with information. It often had to filter through many channels, and sometimes these involved both Christians and Jews. Whatever the case, these channels of communication were amazingly efficient.

Through one of them we soon learned that Josef had been taken to the concentration camp not far from Lublin, called Majdanek.

To succeed then in getting a Jew released from a concentration camp was unheard of. Throughout discussions of extraordinary schemes involving large sums of money, our friends remained convinced that my father was wasting his time. But he persisted, and finally, after considerable financial sacrifice, a miracle was performed. Josef was released from Majdanek.

Physically he looked better than he had when he returned after the deportation, but in a quite different way he was worse than before. More than ever he behaved as if he cared little about life. He avoided people, remained almost totally silent, and only with great reluctance and very superficially did he describe life in the concentration camp. In the evenings he would sit motionless in a corner of our big empty room, perhaps absorbed in thoughts too heavy for expression, perhaps trying not to think at all. Without being rude, he made it clear that he preferred to be left alone.

Yet my uncle's low spirits went unnoticed by my mother. Her depression vanished. She was determined to enjoy her brother's release to the fullest. Without recognizing the change in him, or simply refusing to acknowledge it, she lavished affectionate attention on him, trying to make him into a happy man again.

The new ghetto, Majdan Tatarski, was located on the outskirts of Lublin close to Majdanek. Before the Jews were taken there the entire area had been enclosed by a double row of barbed wire. When the Jews arrived, special guards were stationed around the perimeter. Most of them were Lithuanians and Ukrainians, Nazi collaborators who had enlisted in the German army. Instead of integrating them into the army, however, the Germans preferred to keep them in separate units. To distinguish them from the regular army they dressed them in black uniforms, and we referred to them as black soldiers. As Nazi collaborators they were particularly zealous in the discharge of their duties, especially when Jews were involved. We learned indeed that their reputation for sadism and vicious anti-Semitism was well deserved. Completely at their mercy, Jews had no appeal against them.

With an identification card in hand, a Jew could leave or enter the ghetto through one of two gates, but this was not a simple matter. The guards would seize on the most trivial thing, such as walking too fast or too slowly or not holding the card properly, and use it as a pretext for a beating, kicks, and even shooting. Only Jews who could prove they worked outside the ghetto could pass through the gate. Because of my family's special employment we were allowed to visit. The long hours and the six-day work week at the factory meant that such trips could occur only rarely.

Majdan Tatarski itself was in sharp contrast to the barbed wire and the threatening, black-uniformed guards. It was a modest development, with houses of two or three rooms, each house surrounded by a small garden. Narrow dirt roads, white fences, and an abundance of greenery gave it a good deal of charm. The general effect was that of a small village, just as it must have been when Polish laborers lived here. We never learned what the Nazis did with the Poles after they moved them out.

Even though there was no indoor plumbing, Majdan Tatarski was an improvement over the cramped and dilapidated quarters the Jews had left behind. But their wounds were too fresh and deep for them to take any pleasure in their new surroundings. All had bitter memories of relatives and friends who had either been taken away by force or murdered before their eyes. Still, the Nazis gave them no time for mourning. They insisted that the Jews they had spared settle down immediately and lead orderly lives in this community, just as they had in the old one. The Nazis offered their usual assurances that the survivors would live undisturbed if they abided by the rules.

The immediate authority for procedural matters was vested in the *Judenrat*, a local Jewish council and so-called advisory body that the Nazis had organized in the process of tightening their control over occupied territory. Through the Judenrat the Nazis issued all their official proclamations, and the Judenrat was responsible for executing all orders affecting the Jews. The Judenrat was cordially hated by all those whose interests it was supposed to represent.

This body was now entrusted with the formation of a Jewish police force. Besides assisting the Judenrat, these police enforced the great number of rules imposed on the ghetto dwellers. Some of those rules had to do with maintaining the pleasant aspect of Majdan Tatarski. Besides keeping the whole community scrupulously clean, the Jews were required to plant and weed the gardens. They became anxious about this duty and preoccupied with the activity, and consequently displayed considerable imagination in their planting of flowers and vegetables. The gardens were not only well kept, they were also beautiful. The Germans made inspections, and awarded prizes for those plots they considered the best designed and maintained. Since they tolerated not the slightest deviation from the rules, an untended garden was considered a serious crime. Far lesser transgressions were also punished, and punishment meant disappearance, which in turn meant death.

While others were being settled in the new ghetto, my family and I were readjusting to life in the chemical factory. Because of our excellent papers we were permitted in certain parts of Lublin proper. The newest and most elegant section was of course forbidden to all Jews, no matter what their employment. In practice, we left the factory only when it was absolutely necessary—papers or no papers, safety was never guaranteed, and we felt safest staying inside.

One day my mother returned from a venture into town in a state of terrible distress. As she was heading back to the factory, a fleet of trucks had passed by, loaded with Jews from outside Lublin. In one of them she recognized Zelda, her youngest sister. When she saw my mother Zelda cried out: "Esther, save me, save me!" Zelda's arms were stretched toward my mother as she kept imploring again and again, "Save me, Esther, save me, save me!" The truck pulled far ahead and my mother could hear no more.

Trying to calm her down, my father promised to inquire. Always unusually resourceful, this time too he managed to achieve the impossible, and learned what had become of Zelda. The Jews in the trucks that had passed my mother had been collected from small towns and brought to Lublin. Some were then selected for the Majdanek concentration camp and the rest were put on freight trains bound for other camps. Zelda had been in the latter group. She and a few others had managed to jump off a moving train. She was now in hiding with Polish peasants. My parents dispatched a Christian messenger with money to these peasants, begging Zelda to come and join us. She refused, believing that she had a better chance to survive in the countryside. After that we had no more communication with her.

With my grandparents, too, despite repeated efforts, we were unable to establish contact. At first we heard that they had both been shot during a raid. Later someone brought the news that they had been seen in a concentration camp. Only one thing was certain: we never saw them again.

The year 1942 was moving toward summer. We continued to live in the huge room in the factory. My parents and my sister worked all day. Only I was too young to be given any kind of responsibility—a fact that I resented. I would have·liked to visit my family during the day, but my father felt that the other workers might object to a child's presence and he told me to stay away.

The factory consisted of a cluster of simple structures, some of them one story and others two stories high, arranged in a half circle. In the back of the half circle were stairs leading to an upper level, on which there was a house divided into a few apartments, and a garden surrounded by a wall. Beyond the wall was a convent that an order of teaching nuns ran as a boarding school for girls.

I found a small opening in the wall from which, unobserved, I could watch the girls at play. To me they seemed so content, so carefree, and I envied them their fun. Did they know that a war was on? At times, as I watched them, I too became engrossed in their games and almost forgot about the war. But the bell that called them back to class called me back to reality, and at such moments I became more acutely aware of my loneliness. These small excursions made me feel, in the end, more miserable than ever. The girls in the boarding school were so near and yet so far. The wall that separated us was thick indeed, and eventually I could not bear to go near it.

My parents were aware of my loneliness and depression, but there was little they could do to comfort me. Then one day my mother told me that many young Jewish girls would be coming to work and live in the factory; sure enough about fifty of them moved into our huge room. They were young, between fifteen and twenty years of age. They came from the ghetto, and all of them had lost their families. Each was given a bed with curtains around it for privacy, so that all of us had an illusion of small separate rooms within the huge one.

These newcomers made a fuss over me, and for a little while I felt less lonely. But with time the novelty wore off, and even though it was lively and pleasant after working hours, I still had to be alone during the entire day. My depression returned more strongly than before. I lost my appetite as well as all interest in my surroundings, and when it became obvious that I was losing weight, day by day, my parents began to worry.

Because it was peaceful in Majdan Tatarski, and in order to improve my state of mind, mother took me there several times for visits. I could see Czuczka, and I could play with other children. Each time I went, my urge to stay was stronger. I found it harder and harder to leave.

One day, casually, Czuczka said to my mother: "I wish I could keep Helka with me. This would make the two of us happy."

"And what if there should be a new deportation, and we lost her?" my mother asked sadly.

Her fears, after all, were justified. One never knew

what the Germans would do or when they would do it. But as my depression grew and I lost more weight, my parents became increasingly concerned about my health. After much hesitation, and despite serious reservations, they agreed that I should move to the ghetto and stay with Czuczka.

I was delighted. It did not matter that Czuczka worked in an office during the day. I knew that she would be happy to devote all her free time to me. I had no doubt that for her I was special, just as she was special for me. Welcoming me with a hug, she said, "Helka, this time there will be no regular lessons—we will only enjoy each other's company."

By now the mood of Majdan Tatarski had undergone a dramatic change. On its surface the ghetto looked tranquil, but it was vibrating with anticipation, anxiety and excitement. It was a community predominantly of young people, most between eighteen and thirty, most of them unattached, and they appeared to be throwing off all social restraints. The breakup of families, the Nazi restrictions, and the imminent danger, all led to an emphasis on the *now*. Refusing to think about the future and its uncertainties these young people focused on the present.

The few older members of the community were neither willing nor able to impose their authority. After all, why should they try? These were perilous times: why should the young not feel free to enjoy themselves as long as they could?

The children formed a tiny minority. As a matter of policy, the Nazis were concentrating on the extermination of Jewish children. Because we were thus in special danger, adults looked upon us as a precious commodity. We came to expect our elders to treat us with special indulgence, and they did. No Jew would have thought of mistreating a child, and almost all of them refrained from even the mildest form of discipline.

And so we were free not only of school but also of

adult supervision. We had no special duties. It was summer. Because there were few of us left, we felt close to each other. We relied on each other for support, for entertainment, and for enlightenment. And there was much we had to be enlightened about!

As a rule little escaped us. We were aware of the social climate in the ghetto. We knew of many sexual liaisons, and we frequently surprised lovers in the act. Naturally we shared all such information, elaborating on it liberally with as many imaginative touches as we could. In our own household, Czuczka's brother would sometimes arrive with a girl; they would disappear into the next room, lock the door, and come out only after an hour or more. Neither the young nor the old in the household said a word, and no one seemed embarrassed. Only I could hardly wait to tell my friends about it.

We children managed to be happy as we roamed the little dirt roads in search of adventure. We spent our days outdoors, constantly on the move. In the evenings we took turns visiting each other's houses. In the process we made many exciting discoveries about life, love, and our fellow mortals.

One house in particular we enjoyed—the house where our friend Hanka lived. Hanka was an accomplished pianist, as the Germans knew, and sometimes they would summon her to entertain them and their guests. They even provided her with a piano of her own, the only one in the ghetto.

We loved to gather at Hanka's. She would play both popular and classical music for us, and we would join her in singing. We were all aware of the special value of these gatherings. Without being able to express it in words, we felt that our relatively carefree existence could not last much longer. We knew that we lived in a dangerous and unstable world, but we preferred not to talk about it. Did we think that the danger would go away if nobody mentioned it? Or was the situation simply too frightening for discussion?

The Jewish collaborators were among the signs that in a very real sense our world had been turned upside down. As a rule they were underworld figures who had been invisible before the war. In the ghetto they were very much in evidence, parading their newly acquired wealth and power. All of us hated and feared them, and avoided them as much as possible.

One such notorious figure was a man named Graier. It was rumored that before the war he made his living as a pimp. With the arrival of the Germans his fortunes changed dramatically. He turned collaborator. By means of denunciations and by aiding the Nazis in the dispossession of wealthy Jews, he became rich and powerful, a fact that he displayed without shame.

He was a dark-haired man of medium height with an athletic build and regular features; he dressed only in well-made white or beige suits, which enhanced his good looks and his resemblance to Rudolph Valentino.

He had a mistress, Golda, to whom he was devoted, who was generally believed to have been one of his chief prostitutes. It was hard to imagine how she could have earned money by selling her favors. Unlike Graier, she had a slack and clumsy body, and when she moved one had the feeling that each part of her body was struggling to go in a different direction from the others. Her face, too, was unattractive, with fishlike eyes and irregular features. Even a generous application of makeup could not conceal the fact that she was considerably older than her lover. Ill matched as they seemed, Graier and Golda were the best-known, best-fed, and best-dressed couple in Majdan Tatarski.

Soon an unusual event drastically changed their lives. One day, as Graier was standing at the ghetto gate talking to a group of Gestapo officers, a beautiful girl of seventeen named Mina passed by, returning from work with a group of other Jews. Mina's father was a professor of history and highly respected, but she and her family were then living in abject poverty. No doubt struck by her beauty, one of the Nazis pointed to Mina and said to Graier, "You will make her your wife. You are well suited to each other."

Such an order had to be obeyed and promptly. The lavish wedding that soon ensued was attended by other collaborators and by some Nazi officials. None of Mina's friends came to the wedding; none had been invited.

When the news about Mina's marriage reached us, we expected that she would be miserable, and we felt deeply sorry for her. But things turned out differently. As Graier's wife, Mina was relieved from work and free to concentrate on clothes and amusement. She looked content and happy and more dazzlingly beautiful than ever. In public she displayed much affection toward her husband. We were at first disappointed, and then outraged; pity turned into contempt, contempt into hate. We understood why she had obeyed a Nazi order, but we could not forgive her for being happy about it. She was no longer one of us. She had become one of them.

In the little house in which I lived with Czuczka and her family, there also lived an agricultural expert named Stach. He was a tall, good-looking man, with dark hair and intelligent black eyes. There was an overall sadness about him that never left him, even when he smiled. Mixed with his sadness was a touch of resignation. I learned that during the last raid his wife, who was eight months pregnant, had been beaten to death by a Nazi right in front of his eyes. According to Czuczka, the image of his dying wife was always with him.

Yet he was not bitter, but kind, eager to help in

whatever way he could. When he was doing someone a favor, when he worked in our garden—that was when he smiled.

During the day he had a laborer's job outside the ghetto. His evenings he devoted to our garden. His love for gardening coupled with his great fund of agricultural knowledge transformed our garden into a showpiece. We even won several prizes from the German inspectors. I enjoyed helping Stach and listening to what he said about plants. He treated each one as if it had a personality of its own. He referred to me as his little assistant. I was grateful for his company, eager for his approval.

Frequently, as we worked and chatted, Czuczka would join us. Sometimes Stach, Czuczka, and I would go for a walk. I walked between them, holding each one's hand. They both spoke softly, including me in their conversation and trying to make it interesting for me. They never talked down to me. They gave me a feeling of importance. Those were precious moments; I was acutely conscious of their value, knowing they would not last.

The friendship they felt for me and for each other I valued highly. I observed them and I understood enough to know that they cared for each other in two different ways. Quietly and tenderly, Czuczka was in love with Stach, but she never made her love known. Stach respected Czuczka and appreciated her as a friend. He talked to her, confided in her more than in anyone else, wanted her support and her understanding, and needed her for comfort. But he did not love her as a woman.

I was impressed by the depth of their friendship. Compared to the many fleeting sexual liaisons around us, theirs was a pure relationship, which I was convinced sex would have changed. I considered what they had infinitely more important and more lasting than any love affair could possibly have been.

I was aware that other women tried to press their attentions on Stach. Sometimes they would come and interrupt our work in the garden, and I got angry with them; angry that they dared to intrude, that they were trying to spoil something so precious to me. I was glad that Stach did not encourage them. Interpreting his lack of interest as an act of faithfulness to Czuczka, I was grateful that our friendship could continue untouched by the distractions of our surroundings.

For a while the summer of 1942 went along without any major disasters. Then one afternoon my mother came to Czuczka's house, very upset. She had heard disturbing rumors and wanted to take me back to the factory. She insisted that I would be safer there. The prospect of leaving all my friends and Czuczka as well was unbearable, and I pleaded with my mother to let me stay at least until the next day so I would have time to say good-bye to everyone. I cried until she agreed, saying she would stay with me at Czuczka's until the morning. That night I lay silently beside my mother, feeling angry and sorry for myself. I had been having such a good time. What did she want from me? Why didn't she leave me alone?

My questions were soon answered. At about four in the morning mother shook me violently out of my sleep. "Hurry, Helka, hurry, there is no time, we must hide." Someone had come to warn us that there was going to be a partial liquidation of the ghetto. Children and the elderly were as always in particular danger. I did not need to ask questions, and in no time I was ready.

My mother grabbed me by the hand and ran across the street to the house of friends who had a special hiding place, a skillfully camouflaged cellar. Breathless, we knocked, and my mother begged for admittance. But there was no room there. They were crowded, sitting virtually on top of each other. They could not take us. "Save at least the child, please," my mother pleaded. They refused, suggesting another place. Frantically my mother ran, dragging me along. I could not keep up with her. Twice I fell and got up again, not daring to complain. We knocked at a number of doors, all in vain. But my mother had courage. She did not give up easily. She ran, she almost flew. She knew many people, and she was convinced that someone would help. On our way we passed a few baby carriages in full view, babies inside. They was no place for them. No one would allow them into hiding for fear they would cry and lead to the discovery of others.

At last mother's pleas were heard, and I found myself squeezed into a cramped cellar where I almost had to sit on someone's head. There was no place for my mother, so she left me there. I learned later that only at the last minute did she find shelter.

Soon loudspeakers blared that all Jews were to come out of their houses and into the square. The voice went on to add that farmers were needed in recently reclaimed lands, and that those selected would work the land and lead good lives. This announcement was followed by a thorough search of every house, and many people were removed. When the Aktion was over the population had been reduced to a fraction of what it was. Again, an unusually large proportion of those taken were older people, women, and children. Many were killed immediately. All the babies in carriages were shot, and so were some adults who made a desperate attempt at running away. A friend of my mother's tried to escape through an opening in the barbed wire, holding a child in her arms. She was shot at by a Ukrainian guard and the child, a boy, was killed. Half crazed, she was pushed into the group for deporation, clinging to the dead child. She was deported, still holding him in her arms.

Only after some hours did the people with whom I had hidden allow me to leave. I walked out into a deserted, lifeless street. When I looked into the first baby carriage I saw an unrecognizable bloody mass, that seemed strangely alive. I felt weak and dizzy. All curiosity left me and all courage as well. I began to run, trying to avoid the bloodstained baby carriages and the bodies scattered in every direction on the ground. I felt all the dead were trying to keep me there with some terrifying, inexplicable power. I had to get away.

I burst into Czuczka's house, straight into my mother's outstretched arms. Only so close to her was I able to let myself cry. Then, relieved, I noticed that Stach, Czuczka, and her family were all there too. I stopped crying, but there was no happiness in our reunion. Once again without asking questions, I began to pack. This time I knew that my departure was inevitable, and I felt numb with guilt for having caused my mother so much pain and anxiety.

I expected her to reproach me. Instead she said tenderly, almost in a whisper, "Helka, I am so grateful that you are alive. Maybe there is a God after all!" I felt too miserable and ashamed of myself to answer.

A few people stopped by for a brief moment to see if we had been spared, and to tell us of the disasters that had befallen so many others. Almost all of those I cared about were gone; there would be no point in looking for them.

Czuczka and Stach watched as I silently got ready to go. I could not bear the idea of having to say good-bye to them at that public ghetto gate, and it was as if Czuczka had read my mind. "Let us part here," she said, "not at the gate."

First I embraced Czuczka's parents and brother. Then I turned to Stach. After a strong, almost desperate hug, he took my face into his hands, looked straight into my eyes, and said very seriously: "Promise me always to be brave. Don't ever give up. Ever!" I nodded, feeling a lump in my throat, and turned to Czuczka. I held on to her with all my strength. If I hurt her she did not show it. I lost control and began to cry bitterly. I could not let go of her. I felt her body tremble, and she too began to cry openly—Czuczka, whom I had never seen cry before.

My mother's hand was on my shoulder: "We must go. Surely you will see them again soon." I did not believe her. I felt my mother did not believe herself. Inside me was a painful void and with it came the strong conviction that I would never see any of them again.

Still crying, I followed my mother into the street. When I turned, Czuczka and Stach were standing just as I had left them. I was blinded by my tears and unable to make out their faces. Quickly I wiped my eyes with the palms of both my hands, but just as quickly, before I had a chance to see them one last time, I turned away.

My mother, her shoulders stooped, walked in front of me. As we neared the ghetto gate, she lovingly reached for my hand. I was overcome by a wave of sad tenderness. "Oh, Mama, how good it is to have you!" I thought.

Majdan Tatarski was behind me. I had spent only a few months there, but the time seemed much longer. I had learned so much about life, made so many friends, received so much attention and love. It had been a period tightly packed with meaningful impressions and events, and everything that had happened had touched me deeply. Perhaps it was the significance and fullness of life that made those few months seem to stretch out in memory as if they had been years. But now they were over, and all I felt was pain and sadness.

This time no one worried about my well-being. Survival was the only consideration, and my parents were convinced that the factory was a good place to work. There was enough food for everybody and the treatment was humane.

I was eager to find something to do. I was barely eleven, small and skinny and still too young for a job. My father urged me to read, and out of nowhere managed to provide me with a succession of Polish classics. Because I had nothing else to do, I divided my time among keeping house, reading, and roaming through the garden. I became friendly with a Polish chemist named Bronek and his wife, Genia, who lived in the house in the garden. Genia, in particular, enjoyed having me around. She liked to hug me, and whenever she did she would say, with pleasure and wonderment, "You are such a lovely child, not Jewish at all, not at all."

I never knew my parents to visit this Polish couple, but they must have been in touch with them somehow. I learned from my mother that Genia could not have children and that it made her unhappy. Eventually my mother made an announcement: "Helka, you are a lucky girl. Bronek and Genia want to adopt you!" She spoke joyously, but I felt no joy at all: how could she be happy at the prospect of giving me to strangers? Fortunately for me, my mother's initial enthusiasm waned. She and my father came to feel that too many people around us knew who I was, and that even if I could pass as Bronek's and Genia's daughter in the world at large, one of our acquaintances would eventually betray me.

The mother superior from the convent adjoining our factory was also ready to accept me as one of her charges. This was both generous and courageous of her, because if she took in a Jewish child she ran the risk of the death penalty. My parents were afraid that the convent's nearness to the factory would make it as unsafe for me as the Polish couple's house, so they did not take advantage of the nun's offer, either.

In the meantime life went on with the appearance of normality. Most of us refused to be permanently depressed. In the evenings, when we were all together, we laughed and sang and indulged in lively gossip. The Jewish prisoners were still in Lublin and, surprisingly, many of them managed to get passes to visit the factory. Romantic involvements and even marriages ensued. My parents became more tolerant and agreed that my sister's old admirer might visit her.

At the time it was rare for a Jew to command the respect of a German. One such exception was the respect and trust that existed between my father and the commissioner. Clever and tactful, my father knew how to keep his distance and how not to intrude on others. He was deliberately undemanding, and went out of his way not to take advantage of the commissioner's regard and friendship. At the same time, as in his dealings with everyone else, he retained his dignity and never assumed a subservient position. It was precisely these qualities in my father that the commissioner valued, and they were largely responsible for the special relationship between the two men.

Throughout the war years my father made a conscious effort not to be a leader and not to be responsible for the actions of others. This was not easy for him, because he was accustomed to giving orders, and people obeyed him willingly. Sometimes I heard him explain to his friends: "These are perilous times. No one knows what decisions are right or wrong. I must take the responsibility for my own family, for better or worse. As for others—how can I give them advice when I don't know if it is good or bad?"

While disasters were multiplying, many Jews could not or would not think about the future. Perhaps they were overwhelmed and paralyzed by events. Fortunately, my father was a fighter. He emphasized that passivity could mean disaster. He had been convinced almost from the start that the Germans were bent on our destruction. He felt that the only way we could survive was to hide our identity by passing as Poles. He was preparing for this eventuality, not just for the four of us but for Josef and Czuczka as well.

After my return from the ghetto we never visited it again, but kept in touch with Czuczka through the few Jewish workers who came from the ghetto to work in the city. I was glad to hear that despite the cost and risk, my parents were arranging to buy papers for Czuczka. By then her father had been deported, and her brother was taking care of their mother. Only at her mother's insistence did Czuczka agree to join us when the time came. As for my Uncle Josef, he was the only one of our relatives left, and my parents were determined to help him no matter what the price.

I learned about these plans when our distant cousin Bolek arrived at the factory to help my father with his preparations for a move into the Christian world. Bolek's visit lasted only two days, during which he and my father spent a great deal of time alone together. I did see him from time to time, enough to know that he was very different from the way I remembered him. Some of his carefree manner was gone. He was more serious and also more sure of himself, and one could see at a glance that he was prosperous and lived well. Yet toward my father he showed the accustomed deference and admiration.

I remembered Bolek as a happy-go-lucky fellow, always ready to joke and bubbling with stories about his failures and successes. His carefree ways and his rich, childlike fantasies made him very appealing to my sister and me and we always enjoyed his visits— which generally occurred when his fortunes were at low ebb.

Before the war Bolek had been a marginal character, moving from one occupation to another, living
mostly on dreams and borrowed money. His last job,
which involved selling ties on the street corners, got
him his nickname, Krawaciarz, Bolek the "Tie Man."
All of his other relatives refused to have anything to
do with him, but my father accepted him and treated
him with kindness. Whenever Bolek was in need of
help, he knew he could count on my father. He felt
close to him and looked up to him. After each of his
financial reverses he would solemnly promise to follow my father's advice to the letter. This of course he
never did, nor did my father expect him to.

My mother did not share my father's affection or
our own youthful enthusiasm for Bolek. She remained
puzzled that her husband could take an interest in
such a "drifter," even though she acknowledged he
was a charming one. But puzzled or not, she too
always welcomed him. She liked to help the needy
and needy Bolek surely was, almost every time he
visited us.

The war, which brought drastic and terrible changes
for so many of those we knew, wrought a marvelous
change for Bolek. He became a success. He was
befriended by high German officers, through whom
he became a prosperous wheelerdealer. We never
really knew what he did. We only knew he lived in
style in Warsaw, and we heard from him only sporadically. Now, in 1942, he had come to help us, and
in a way to repay us for all the kindness we'd shown
him.

After his visit, my father explained Bolek's mission.
He was to help us get new identification papers and
then to become established on "the Aryan side,"
meaning any part of a city, town, or village that was
off limits to Jews. My father went on to explain that
Jews who wanted to pass were safer in small groups,
thereby minimizing the risk of discovery. Those who

looked least Jewish obviously had the best chance of passing. In our family my father and I looked most Christian, my sister only a little less so, but my mother was unmistakably Jewish. There was the additional complication of my parents' Polish. Their poor grammar and their inflection would surely betray them.

These were serious obstacles. In order to go into hiding, my parents therefore had to find a Polish family willing to provide them with the necessary cover. My father and mother would have to become in effect invisible by living with such a family. Their false identification papers could be used only in emergencies, if they had to move from place to place. In contrast, there was little reason for my sister and me to go into seclusion. Because of our appearance, and because our Polish was flawless, we could lead relatively normal lives. But because we both were young, my sister fifteen and I eleven, we too would have to live with a Polish family. Whether we should stay with our parents could not be decided ahead of time. Everything depended on whether we could find even one such Polish family. Moreover, none of these plans were feasible in Lublin, where we all ran the risk of being identified and denounced.

The first step, in any event, was to obtain Polish identification papers. There were different kinds of false papers. The best carried the name of some living person. The difficulty lay in selecting such a person and making sure that he or she had moved far away. One then arranged to take out a duplicate birth certificate in that person's name. On the basis of the birth certificate one could obtain other documents—which, however, only adults needed. These, in a sense, were "real" papers, as opposed to a wholly counterfeit kind that carried the name of a fictitious person. Those were manufactured by special printers and were known under the special name of "lipa." There were of course poor forgeries and good ones.

Both the "real" and the counterfeit could be purchased from people who specialized in these matters, and as a rule such people were to be found in Warsaw.

No matter how good the papers, a Jew carrying them was in constant danger of denouncement—and denouncement almost invariably meant death. Intense interrogation easily revealed inconsistencies between the background indicated in the papers and the replies given by the person under interrogation. Even if no such inconsistencies emerged, there was still the question of religion. There was so much a good Catholic had to know that a Jew could hardly avoid making some slip. And for a man, even emerging from the interrogation unscathed was not enough. No Christian Poles were circumcised. A simple physical check was enough to doom a Jew.

This was the summer of 1942. We had lived under the Nazis for three years and could not help but realize that for us time was running out. The German commissioner at the factory was frank, and at considerable risk to himself he warned us that he might not be allowed to keep us much longer—that the danger in fact was imminent.

At the same time the Germans kept circulating announcements that promised the Jews tranquility and peace if they volunteered for deportation to the East. All volunteers would be provided with land on which they could live and work peacefully as farmers. To some the picture thus painted was tempting. The idea of resettling in the East appealed, for instance, to my father's former business partner Moshe, who had lost his fighting spirit. He came to argue his case with my father. "Let us all go together," he pleaded. "After all, don't you want peace? What is the point of running? The Germans are offering us a good chance to survive the war."

My father would not hear of it. "I don't trust them," was all he said. "They will have to come and get me."

Moshe finally changed his mind: he did not register either, and so at least for the moment he was
spared.

Our papers, which at last arrived from Warsaw,
carried fictitious names..But they looked undeniably
authentic, and we were happy to have them. We now
confronted the all but insurmountable obstacle of
leaving Lublin, where too many people knew us too
well. Jews were not allowed to travel; we had heard
of people being taken off trains and shot, and my
mother would be readily identified as Jewish. After
much deliberation, we decided that she would travel
disguised as a woman in mourning. The fashion of
the day for elegant Polish women in mourning was
to dress entirely in black, including a hat with a thin
black veil that covered the face. No Jews ever dressed
this way, a factor that we believed would make the
disguise all the more effective. And to avoid the risk
she ran because of her faulty Polish, my mother
began trying to teach herself how to keep silent. We
had also arranged with Bolek to send a Pole to accompany us on the train when the time came.

We were still involved in our final preparations,
exchanging frequent messages with Bolek, as summer came to an end. There was danger in the air.
More raids took place in Majdan Tatarski. In one of
them Stach was taken away for no apparent reason.
Those of us living in the factory remained untouched,
but we knew that this could not last.

The final hour arrived at the beginning of November, 1942. Lublin was proclaimed *Judenrein*, clean
of Jews. At dawn the commissioner came to tell us
that the ghetto was being liquidated. "In a matter of
hours they will be coming for you, too," he went on.
"Save yourselves as best you can." Panic ensued, and
all of us began frantically dressing and packing. Most
of those who had shared the huge room with us ran
away; the rest seemed too stunned to move, and in a

paralysis of the will simply stayed at the factory, waiting to be rounded up. Both for those who stayed and for those who ran, the chances of survival were slim. There were no places to hide for the majority of those who did run, and they were later picked up in various parts of the city.

We were more fortunate. Some time before, my father had transferred ownership of his candle factory to his former employee, Mr. Pys, with whom he had long been on friendly terms. He had also left Mr. Pys many valuable household items, including crystal, silver, and expensive china. Grateful for what he had received, and also for the trust my parents had in him, Mr. Pys had agreed to our taking refuge in his home if events forced us to leave the factory. The time had come to take advantage of his offer—a generous one indeed, for by taking us in he would put himself and his family in jeopardy. The Nazis were explicit: the penalty for hiding Jews was death.

Josef was still at the factory, and my parents urged him to come with us. He refused. My mother cried and pleaded, but to no avail. He argued that five people trying to escape in a group would never survive. "Only alone do I have a chance," he told my mother. His argument made sense, all the more so because his Polish was flawless. It was natural that he should feel safer alone.

Of the four of us, my mother went first, accompanied to the Pys apartment by a trustworthy Polish factory worker. She was dressed, as planned, as a Polish lady in mourning. No one recognized her, and no one would have taken her for a runaway Jew. My sister went next, going with another worker we trusted. My father and I left together, a few minutes after my sister.

Even though the arrangements had been made in advance, the Pys family was not overjoyed by our arrival. Mrs. Pys's mother, who lived with them, had been born a Jew and had converted to Catholicism as a little girl. The family was fearful that if the Germans discovered her origins that alone would place them in real danger—and our presence put them in double jeopardy. They made it plain that they regretted their offer of help.

Father tried to calm them by assuring them that we had no intention of staying long. Indeed, through Bolek's efforts we were already in close touch with the young Pole who had come to lead us out of Lublin. But for the time being it was best to stay in the house. The Nazis' intensive search for Jews extended beyond the streets and the ghetto. They were conducting inspections at the railroad station, within the trains, and at every stop, all the way to Warsaw. In this way they trapped many fleeing Jews, and they kept looking for more.

Through the windows of Mr. Pys's apartment we could hear the constant shout of *"Jude, Jude!"* We dared not show our faces, and withdrew to a small room at the back of the apartment. While we waited for the immediate crisis to pass, the guide sent by Bolek went off to meet Czuczka at a particular house in the outskirts of Lublin.

He came back without her. He had found her only because no one had bothered to bury her. She was lying on the ground beside the house in which she had been hiding, her hair disarrayed, her glasses missing, and without eyes. The birds had attended to her body. The picture he drew was vivid and merciless. We were spared no details. This image of her lying there, murdered, alone, and without eyes, haunted me for a long, long time.

As we waited to leave we memorized our new names. We needed to know not only our own, of course, but those of our parents, just as we needed to know our dates of birth and the place where our papers said we had been born. My new name was Pelagia Pawlowska. According to these forged papers we were all unrelated strangers, the idea being that if one of us was discovered the others would still have a chance of passing. We also tried to memorize Catholic prayers, a precautionary measure in case the police questioned us about our religion.

In the meantime, the guide whom Bolek sent from Warsaw stood by awaiting my parents' orders. To minimize the danger it was agreed that my sister would go first, and the guide would take her to Bolek's place in Warsaw. My parents would follow, traveling in the same train but in different compartments. They felt that it would be too dangerous for me to go with them, arguing that if they were killed on the way at least I would survive. Because of my fair hair and blue eyes and my command of Polish I stood the best chance of survival; they did not want to risk destroying it by taking me with them. They would send for me later. I felt miserable and dejected, but did not object. Everything was explained, everything made sense. It was a painful decision for all of us. I was not going to prolong our agony by arguing.

Our hosts were unhappy about having me stay longer with them. Mrs Pys and her mother in particular did nothing to hide their distress. Mr. Pys agreed only reluctantly, and only with the understanding that my parents would send for me as soon as possible.

We all knew the possibility that my parents would not survive was real. It was understood that if they were killed the Pys family would be stuck with me. They had two children of their own and were not anxious to have another, particularly a Jewish child. In fact, it was to their credit that they agreed, no matter how reluctantly, to go along with this arrangement.

Then Mr. Pys brought us the tragic news about my Uncle Josef. After we left him, Josef hid in the factory's warehouse. Some Polish workers discovered him and denounced him. He was shot on the spot by the Gestapo.

My sister left for Warsaw. Days passed before we heard from her and learned what had happened. On the way she had been taken off the train and interrogated, but she put on what must have been a convincing show of indignation when questioned about her name, the date and place of her birth, the names and whereabouts of her parents, and her religion. Having the Polish guide with her helped. He claimed to be her fiancé, and in the end she was released. For the present, she was safe with Bolek.

The night came for my parents' departure. They decided to take a late train. There was safety in darkness. As the hours passed into the night, I desperately tried to overcome my tiredness. Gently, my parents urged me to go to sleep, promising that they would wake me in time to say good-bye. I was too tired and too miserable to resist. I went to bed.

Startled, I woke up. My father was bending over me, a strangely intense look on his face that I had never seen before. It took me a moment to remember where I was and what was happening. This was the Pys apartment, and it was time to say good-bye to my parents. They were leaving for Warsaw without me.

I felt something wet. Father's tears were on my face. Desperately and impulsively, I threw my arms around him, and before I could help myself I sobbed, "Take me with you, don't leave me, please don't leave me!" Immediately I was ashamed of my outburst. I knew my parents were leaving me only because they wanted me to be safe and that it was wrong of me to cause them more suffering.

My mother, crying without a sound, stood beside my father. He looked at me for a moment, shaken and in pain. "Dress quickly," he said. "You are taking the train with us!" He turned to my mother: "There is no point in leaving her here. What kind of a life will she have here when we are dead? Let her come."

My blond hair carefully combed, I dressed with special neatness. I was given a doll to carry so that I would look even more like a Polish child. My mother in her mourning clothes, her face hidden behind the veil, would be with me, but my father would travel in a different train compartment. Our plan was to sit next to a window, and at each stop my father would tap on it twice to let us know that he was still alive.

No one tried to stop my mother and me as we walked to the station, some distance ahead of my father. I wanted to look behind me, to make sure that no one had stopped him, but of course my mother and I had to behave as though we did not even know he existed. When we had safely reached the station we walked along the platform, tightly holding hands, looking for a compartment with a window seat still vacant. When we found one, the temptation to look back, to see if my father was watching, almost overwhelmed me. But trying to appear calm, I boarded the train without having turned my head.

As we seated ourselves, the train jolted into motion and pulled slowly, slowly out of the station. The passengers hardly looked at my mother, but I did draw their attention. They seemed to go out of their way to be kind to me. Some patted me on the head, some offered me candy, and some even tried to engage me in conversation. My mother never let go of my hand. Her grip was desperate, full of meaning.

We did not speak to each other. Only the pressure of hands and bodies was there.

At each stop we waited. And at each stop, against the window came the double tap.

Despite my apprehension I was happy. I was relieved at being beside my mother and close to my father. They did not leave me behind, I kept thinking, and the train wheels seemed to click out the same words: They did not leave you behind, they did not leave you behind.

Behind me was Lublin, the city in which I was born —a city now *Judenrein*.

CHAPTER TWO

———◆●▶———

My World Before

LUBLIN is an ancient city that assumed a dominant position in Poland as early as the fourteenth century. The old, run down, and neglected part of the city was dominated by a castle, built sometime after 1300, that stood on a hilltop and was surrounded by massive stone walls. It must have been an imposing place when it was the home of the fourteenth-century king, Kazimierz the Great. Of its past glory, however, only its size remained. For centuries after Kazimierz it had served as a prison and had acquired the appropriately gloomy appearance. Around and close to its walls were old one-story buildings, some of them used as living quarters, some as shops. Huddled together, sturdy still, but badly in need of paint and repair, they formed an extended but uneven circle, broken by narrow winding cobblestone streets. For much of the day the sunlight barely penetrated there. The further removed from the ancient castle the buildings stood, the better their appearance and the more livable they were as houses.

Eventually the uneven circle of streets and buildings ended, and with it ended the old city of Lublin. The newer part of town adjoining the old one was made up of small factories, craft shops, stores, and homes. More desirable than the old part, it was by no means the best. The third and best section of town was built on the opposite side of the old city. It had two beautiful parks, wide streets, modern buildings, and elegant shops.

As Polish cities went, Lublin was a big one. About one fifth of its 200,000 citizens were Jews, most of whom preferred to live in the ghetto area in the old city. The more prosperous Jews and those who wanted to assimilate lived in the modern and predominantly Christian section. My parents had moved to this part of Lublin when I was still an infant.

My father, who was a dominant figure in my life, was twenty-seven when I was born. He was a complex man with uncommon ideas about Jewishness and religion. Early in life he had been groomed for the rabbinate. He was an outstanding student at the yeshiva in Lublin, which was famous for its high standards of learning. There he acquired a reputation for his precociously critical probing into the meanings and implications of religion.

On his own, and against the wishes of his teachers, he studied the cabbala, a mystical medieval work. He began to question his teachers. Their answers did not satisfy him. He was told to ask less and trust more. He refused. Eventually there was an outright confrontation between him and his teachers, which brought his religious instruction to an end.

Once he had left the yeshiva, he went out of his way to defy traditional religious practices. On Yom Kippur, the Day of Atonement, when all Jews are supposed to fast, he made no attempt to restrain his appetite. Even more shocking, he ate ham and other non-kosher foods on this, the most solemn day of all, as well as the rest of the high holidays. He also enjoyed telling stories that ridiculed the hypocrisy of religious Jews.

But even though he considered himself an atheist, his excursions into Christian practices did not disturb the traditional order of our household. My mother kept a kosher home, she lighted candles, said the required prayer, and served a traditional dinner. And when my father wanted to eat ham, as indeed he often did, it was served on special dishes.

No doubt it was my mother's particular approach to religion that accounted for my father's lack of interference with her practices. She was an "instinctive" Jew, who behaved in a religious way naturally and without thought. Observing the various rituals was second nature to her, and she was sincere about them. When it came to religion, she never tried to convince anyone or to prove anything. She did what she did because she did not understand what else to do. She never explained to me or my sister what it meant to be Jewish or how we should feel about ourselves as Jews. That part of our education was left entirely to my father.

Early in life I became aware of my "non-Jewish" appearance. Blond and blue-eyed, I had what was considered to be a "typically Polish" look. I knew that this formed a kind of protection and that other Jews were less fortunate than I.

I heard about young Polish anti-Semites who roamed the streets, beating up Jews for no reason except that they were Jews. Eventually I saw for myself such youths parading in front of Jewish businesses, breaking windows, shouting out savage slogans: "Don't buy from the dirty Jew! Jews are bloodsuckers! Jews are thieves! Jews are Christ killers!"

When such attacks occurred all business stopped. Neither Jews nor Poles dared enter a store surrounded by an anti-Semitic mob. As a rule, at such times the police managed to be out of sight.

For me these episodes had a strange fascination. Instead of avoiding them, I wanted to see them, feeling that if I managed to appear calm, the youths would not identify me as Jewish. Yet as I looked on, pretending indifference, I shuddered inwardly. Fear, anger, disgust, and, strangely enough, a strong feeling of satisfaction were all a part of my reaction. Why the satisfaction? I had *fooled* the enemy. I was smarter than they because they did not recognize the Jew in me. They were not so powerful after all!

I grew up with the idea that Jews were despised, and that they suffered only because of their Jewishness. Unobtrusively and indirectly, my father explained to me his understanding of what it meant to be a Jew. He pointed out that a person's birth was a matter of chance, and that there was no reason to be either proud or ashamed of what one had been born. Jews suffered because of such a chance occurrence, and to avoid suffering they had to assimilate. I came to understand that for my father assimilation by its very nature had to be a slow and gradual process, a process free of urgency. But although he favored assimilation, he also insisted that Jews should not deny their origin.

These ideas I accepted automatically, without thought. I was not bothered by the fact that my father never told me how I could assimilate without denying my origin. I failed to notice the contradiction. "Sometime," I thought, "in the distant future, I will become a full-fledged Pole."

I knew that my parents could never become fully assimilated. They were too "Jewish," not so much because of their physical appearance as because of an array of other identifying traits. Yiddish was the language they had been born to, and their knowledge of Polish was limited.

Yiddish brought in its wake special inflections, expressions, and sentence structures. And these, in turn, were accompanied by certain facial expressions, gestures, and movements that Christian Poles considered "typically Jewish."

Jews themselves did not approve of these special Jewish characteristics. My parents made a conscious effort to keep my sister and me from acquiring them.

They spoke to us only in Polish, even though they were much more fluent in Yiddish. Whenever I showed an interest in Yiddish, my father discouraged it by telling me that Yiddish was not a true language, and that it was more important for me to know Polish. And so, to please him, I stuck to Polish. Furthermore, instead of calling me by my Hebrew name, Nechama, they gave me the Polish name, Hela, with Helka as a diminutive.

Being in the Christian section of Lublin helped to remove us further from some of the Jewish influences. We lived on Pijarska, which was one of the side streets off the most attractive avenue in Lublin, Krakowskie Przedmiescie. Our apartment was on the second floor. A small anteroom led into a kitchen, which in turn led into a combination dining room and living room. In the middle of this large bright room stood a massive table surrounded by twelve equally massive chairs. This was the center for all family activities, for reading, and for entertainment.

We had electricity and running water—which in itself was a sign of progress. Many houses, especially those in the ghetto and some in the newer part of Lublin, had no running water and even lacked electricity. I knew of no house that had central heating or used electricity or gas for cooking. Our kitchen, like most others, had a stove built of brick and tile that burned wood or coal. In the winter the rest of the apartment was heated by special stoves built into the walls, each of which had to be individually tended.

Because of its location, most of the tenants in our apartment house were Christians, and yet the only neighbors we knew were Jews. Our Christian neighbors, both adults and children, were complete strangers to me. I never wondered why this was so, nor was I ever upset by it. Indeed only later did I realize that although I lived in the Christian section of the city, I had never succeeded in entering the Christian world.

I liked our quiet and subdued neighborhood, but

I also enjoyed visiting other parts of the city. The bustle, the crowding, the loud and varied noises of the old city had a special attraction for me. So did the local market, situated on a slope and covering a vast area, which served as a link between the old and newer parts of Lublin. It was a noisy and wonderfully lively place, overflowing with manufactured goods as well as produce brought in by local farmers driving horsedrawn wagons—milk and cheese and butter, fresh vegetables and fruit, as well as handwoven cloth, wooden shoes, and pottery.

As a preschooler I loved to accompany my mother to this place. Because she suffered from a chronic sinus condition she could taste nothing, and took me along to help her select the freshest produce. She believed that only the best was good enough for my father, and that my sense of taste and smell was highly discriminating. Not infrequently a farmer would eye me with hostility, knowing my decision might mean the loss of a sale. Some of them sneered, or mumbled under their breath that a brat like me knew nothing about quality, but they failed to intimidate me. Sometimes, if the vendor was really unpleasant, I would declare a product unacceptable even when it was good.

During these trips I was particularly fascinated by the professional water carriers. They balanced thick wooden poles across their shoulders, with a pail of water attached at either end. They walked at a special pace, water splashing from the pails, as they warned people to move out of the way. There were also old men carrying sacks on their backs that looked as old as they did, and who called out in sing-song that they would buy old things, any old things, and pay a fantastic price. Unless one knew who they were and had been told ahead of time what they were saying, it was impossible to understand their special chant, and I never knew what they did with the old things they actually bought. Local beggars, too, had a special attraction for me, partly because they were so articulate, and also because they seemed so picturesque. My mother allowed me to give them a few *groszy*. She took their pleas at face value, never doubting that they were desperately in need.

My parents had a great deal of respect for learning. Education, they believed, was an individual's most valuable and durable commodity, to be obtained at any cost. Both of them, though for different reasons, had been forced to interrupt their schooling early, my father because he was orphaned and had to support himself, my mother because her own mother was opposed to education for girls.

No doubt to compensate for their own deprivation, they were determined that my sister and I should get the best education available. They enrolled us in an excellent and expensive private school, owned and run by Jews, and attended exclusively by students from affluent Jewish families. Its entire atmosphere, however, suggested an attempt to de-emphasize anything of religious or particular Jewish significance.

My introduction to the principal was painful. On meeting him I became speechless, clung to my mother and desperately tried to hide behind her. Our awkward encounter ended with his saying, "I hope that you will do as well as your sister." Right then I knew that I would not. Indeed, I saw little point in making an effort. All my parents' emphasis on education made little impression on me. I performed poorly in class, wrote sloppily, and repeatedly failed to hand in homework. Often, too, I woke up in the morning with a stomachache—possibly imaginary, although it seemed real enough to my mother, who would allow me to stay at home.

My father was an unusual man. At the age of fourteen, about the time he became disillusioned with religion, he was also orphaned, which left him without any means of support. I heard stories about cruel relatives who had humiliated him by denying him shelter and aid. Understandably I preferred stories about his successes, which had not come about immediately or easily. They were preceded by many disappointments through years of hard work, during which he had no proper adult supervision and no permanent home. In the course of one of his jobs, as a laborer in a candle factory, he met my mother. She was the owners' daughter, and despite the social distance between them they fell in love. Her parents of course considered this a most unsuitable match. My father was irreligious, homeless, and penniless, combining all the qualities they regarded as objectionable, and his audacity in courting their daughter more than surprised them. My mother was a very pretty girl, and her parents were well-to-do. The dowry that had been set aside for her, her good looks, and her good family, all entitled her to be selective. Her parents proceeded to place many obstacles in the way of the young people's romance. My grandmother in particular voiced strong opposition to such a marriage, and she would have succeeded had it not been for developments beyond her control.

The early days of the Depression came, and with it my grandparents lost their fortune. Of their four daughters, two were already married, and my mother and a younger sister remained at home. Now their dowries had evaporated, and their desirability as marriage partners immediately declined. Stubborn and persistent, my father was still around, willing to marry my mother even though she would not bring him a penny. He became an acceptable match.

After they were duly married, my father promised himself and his bride that they would become rich, and he opened a small candle factory of his own. The established candle manufacturers resented his intrusion, and tried to eliminate him by cutting prices. But my father was no coward, nor was he likely to retreat without a fight. The other manufacturers had to pay for labor, but he did all the work himself, and he could afford to cut prices further than his competitors. A virtual price war followed. It became a war without winners. When all the parties were financially exhausted, they brought it to an end. They agreed that instead of undermining one another's business, they would merge. They formed a syndicate composed of ten factories.

Having proved himself an impressive fighter, my father assumed a controlling voice in the merger. Even though he was the youngest among the partners, the others respected and feared him. But although most people respected him, few became his close friends. He was tactful and trustworthy but not particularly outgoing or warm, always preferring to keep others at a distance.

When I visited our factory, I was proud to see that he was treated as a person of consequence. It was obvious even to me, young as I was, that the workers were loyal to him. And when a labor dispute arose, both his partners and the workers wanted him to arbitrate. He had gained the reputation of being a man people could trust. This trust extended even to burglars. Shortly before the war began, burglars broke into the candle factory and got away with a lot of merchandise. The police were unable to retrieve any of the stolen goods. But a representative of the burglars got in touch with my father and told him that they would return the goods for a fraction of their value, with the stipulation that only my father would be involved in the delicate negotiations. He followed their instructions, paid the sum they demanded, and the losses were reduced to a minimum.

His growing success in the candle business led to success in other areas, and in time he became co-owner of a large chemical factory. Among the products manufactured in this factory were fly paper, shoe polish, soap, plastic boxes, and Christmas decorations. With such a variety of items workers could be kept busy all year around. The factory's very versatility served as an outlet for my father's creativity. He had his own laboratory installed, in which he experimented with new ways of making shoe polish, soap, and many other products. He fancied himself an amateur chemist, but was realistic enough to employ professionals.

As our family became more prosperous, my parents followed what was then a widespread practice among the well-to-do—they took separate vacations, each at a different elegant health resort that seemed suited to their individual needs. For the three summers prior to the war they sent my sister and me to stay with our grandparents and our mother's youngest sister, Zelda, in Naleczow, yet another resort.

During those summers in Naleczow, my grandmother was unmistakably in charge. She was tall and slim, with a beautiful figure and beautiful legs. Her features were regular, her eyes blue and penetrating, and we had been told that she was blond. We never saw her real hair because she was Orthodox, and according to the religious custom had to wear a wig, or *shaitl.*

After my grandparents had lost most of their fortune, they were forced to move from Lublin to a smaller town, Miedzyrzec, where they personally operated a candle factory. My grandfather was a gentle, scholarly man, not well suited to business. In his desire to be fair to customers, he would warn them about possible defects in his products and give them extra weight without extra charge. In contrast, my grandmother loved power and admired success, and was impatient with his ineptitude. But even though she took control of the business they made only a modest living.

I loved my grandfather, and it irritated me that my grandmother did not make him happy. As far as

I knew, she had never even tried to. In accordance with Jewish customs of those days, their marriage had been arranged by the respective parents, who considered the young pair a suitable match. How either of them felt did not matter, and indeed they met for the first time under the *hupa*, the wedding canopy, during the wedding ceremony. According to the story that came down to us, when my grandmother's veil was lifted and she first set eyes on her bridegroom, she fainted.

I often wondered why, because my grandfather was a tall, good-looking man, and at least to me he seemed a sort of unassuming angel, invariably patient, attentive, and understanding. My grandmother, it was explained, had been in love with a cousin whom her parents considered too worldly, and they had forbidden her to marry him. Still, this did not satisfy me. I kept wondering why she had not done all her crying and lamenting before the marriage ceremony. She'd had enough notice.

My mother had four sisters and a brother. Except for the youngest sister, Zelda, they were all married, with children. All the adults in our family wanted Zelda to marry; all except Zelda herself. She was tall, with a well-proportioned figure, but because she had red hair and freckles she was considered unattractive. She was introduced to many eligible men. Those who might have agreed to marry her she dismissed as bores. Often I heard my mother ask angrily, "What do you want, a Prince Charming? With your choosiness, you will end up an old maid." What I saw as courage, others saw as stubbornness that would lead to disaster.

My grandparents' favorite was their only son, Josef. Despite their Orthodoxy, they did not insist that he finish the yeshiva or that he grow a beard and become a pious Jew. They allowed him to follow his inclinations and finish a secular high school, something they denied all four daughters. Money was always available to him even when it meant a sacrifice.

Josef was a good-looking, charming man, easygoing, spoiled, and irresponsible. Unlike his mother, he did not believe in hard work. He owned a jam factory which was established partly with the help of his parents, and partly with the dowry he had acquired when he married. His wife was a beautiful girl, with whom he had two sons. She was not only beautiful, she was also intelligent and pleasant. Yet his wife's special attributes did not alter his interest in other women. On the contrary, he was neither discreet nor selective in his sexual activities.

Even my mother, who generally refused to recognize her brother's shortcomings, was annoyed by his extramarital escapades. I once heard her say: "I hate the way you chase girls all over town. I can do little about that, but in *my* house I want you to stop pinching the maid!" This had little effect. Josef only laughed at her.

My mother, who was about a year older than Josef, had been her parents' third disappointment in a row. Although aware of their attitude, my mother was devoted to her parents. Instead of rebelling she accepted their view of the importance of sons, and her generosity toward her mother and father had no limits.

Happily for my sister and me, my father took a different view of daughters. As far back as I can remember my mother liked telling me the story of my birth. She had been in labor for days when the doctors admitted there was no more they could do. Fearing for my mother's and my life, everyone turned to God. The rabbi conducted special services, with all family members in attendance, and it was only on the fourth day that God decided to listen and I made my official entry into this world.

Exhausted and weak though she was, my mother

insisted on seeing me. But when I was held up above
her head and she knew she had given birth to a
second daughter, she fainted. My father comforted
her. He reminded her that he was not a religious
Jew, said a child was a child, and assured her that he
did not mind my being a girl.

My father had two younger siblings to whom he
was devoted and for whom he felt responsible—a
sister, Ella, and a brother, Gershon. Gershon worked
in my father's candle factory, and on frequent weekends he and his family were guests in our house.

Although my father treated both his brother and
sister with great consideration, he was especially attached to Ella. The age difference between them was
not more than four or five years, but in terms of
strength, self-assurance, and experience they were
worlds apart. Tall and slim, gentle and soft-spoken,
Ella was attractive in a delicate way. Much of the
time she looked a little resigned, a little overwhelmed.
She adored my father. He felt protective toward her
and treated her like a child.

According to my mother, who never tired of telling the story, Ella married not only with my father's
blessing but also with his generous dowry. Szymon,
her husband, was a "professional" socialist, and a
journalist of sorts. He was a short man, with bushy
hair and inquisitive burning eyes. He carried a per-
petual chip on his shoulder, and never missed an
opportunity to attack people who were better off
than he. He was devoted to "truth," especially the
variety that offended his employers. Not surprisingly, he was almost always between jobs. This gave him
time to write articles for Jewish papers, and their
belligerence increased the number of his enemies.

My father supported him and his family with a
steady allowance, for which Szymon refused to be
grateful. To Ella's distress, he even attacked father
as a capitalist and an exploiter of the working class.
He maintained that if his sisters were rich they would

be far more generous than his brother-in-law—a safe assertion, because his sisters had always been in modest circumstances, and remained so.

Fortunately my father expected no gratitude. "You give because of the pleasure it gives you," he said. "Don't ever expect anything in return." Indeed, he seemed uncomfortable when people showed him too much gratitude. One day, for instance, as I entered a room in our apartment, I saw my Aunt Ella accepting money from my father. Abruptly, she bent down and kissed his hand. Even more abruptly, my father freed it. He looked pale, startled, and embarrassed, and seemed to suffer a spasm of great pain and sadness. All this happened in an instant, and without quite understanding why I pretended that I had seen nothing.

Yet my father's generosity was not indiscriminate. Those from whom he had suffered an injustice could expect few favors. But the injustice had to be genuine. The fact that my grandmother strongly disapproved of him and refused to accept him initially as her son-in-law he considered unfortunate but not unjust, at least from her point of view. On the other hand, when he had been homeless and in need of a bed, one of his aunts denied him access to her house. He never forgave her. Much later the same aunt, old, childless, and homeless, turned to him for help. He rented an apartment for her and helped her financially, but he never allowed her into his own house.

On most Friday and Saturday evenings, distant and close relatives and many friends would come to visit us. There was a lot of conversation, during which all the guests would help themselves to cakes, nuts, and sweets, and sip homemade wine and cherry cordials. Children were a part of these gatherings and allowed to eat any of the goodies, but they were not supposed to intrude on adult conversations.

During these evenings, as a rule I had a permanent place on my father's lap. He would stroke my hair, put his arm around me, and from time to time implant a kiss that might land anywhere on my cheek, my brow, the top of my head. It did not matter where to me. Being close to him filled me with contentment. Eight years old, I loved his attentions, and reciprocated with an occasional kiss or hug.

It was during one such gathering that I first heard mention of an impending war. I paid little attention to the idea—or, for that matter, to my mother's worried talk about my Uncle Josef, who could be drafted into the army. She had a reputation as a habitual worrier, not to be taken too seriously. Besides, I had also overheard that my father, who suffered from chronic bronchitis, would be exempt from military duty, and that was enough for me.

At that time I had a governess, whom I saw as a nuisance and as an obstacle to my freedom. When I complained about her, all my mother said was: "It is good for you, it is educational." I never succeeded in convincing my mother that the governess added nothing to my education. Every day the governess took me to the park, where she met other governesses with whom she chatted endlessly, and never paid any attention to me. They, too, talked about the war.

The more talk I heard about war the more I assumed it would be a great adventure. The rumors kept multiplying, and according to the radio we would defeat the Germans. Believing what I heard, I wondered what victory would be like.

Then came Friday, September 1, 1939. My parents left the house telling us that they would be back in the afternoon. My sister and I stayed home. They returned much sooner than expected, with the news that the war had begun. Before we had time to think what this meant, we heard air raid sirens, and even as we moved down to the cellar a bomb exploded.

Our entire building shook and some windows were broken. We learned later that a nearby house had been entirely demolished.

During the next few days the air raid alarms and bombings were almost continuous. I lost track of time. Then I heard the adults around me talk of the German blitzkreig, and say that we were losing the war. I felt they had to be mistaken. The emotional calls to battle and promises of victory that I had heard on the radio were still fresh in my ears. I was convinced that eventually the real truth would come out. Indeed, when the real truth did come out, when the Germans arrived, I was angry. I felt as if someone had lied to me; I felt betrayed.

The Germans were definitely there. Overnight their meticulously clean uniforms and highly polished black leather boots were all over the city. From the start their arrogance was conspicuous. But as yet we had no idea what their presence really meant. After less than a week my father went back to his factories and my sister and I back to school.

Apart from the omnipresent uniforms, life in Lublin went on much as usual. Although rumors began circulating that the Germans intended to do away with all the Jews, there was no evidence to support such assertions. They were fantastic tales, people said, and refused to believe them.

A little later, Jews from part of Poland close to the German border started to arrive, bringing with them few possessions and many stories. At first they were allowed to live anywhere in town, and some even managed to move into our building. These refugees had been thrown out of their homes on no provocation and without warning, and they spoke of many who had been killed before they could get away. Most of our Jewish acquaintances remained stubbornly skeptical, even about these first-hand accounts. Unlike them, my father listened carefully.

Almost every day the Nazis issued new regulations concerning Jewish ownership of stores, factories, and other places of business. Because of the mounting uncertainty about the future, my father and his partners decided to disband the candle factory syndicate. Each took his machinery and set up on his own, believing that a small operation would stand a better chance of escaping a German takeover.

As the Nazi presence in Lublin grew, increasing numbers of Jews came to believe that the Russians might be the lesser of two evils. Some of them crossed illegally into the Russian part of Poland, leaving their families behind with the intention of returning to fetch them if they found the situation suitable. Among those who left was my father's brother. He, among many others, was unable to return. He would survive in Russia, while the wife and son he had left behind would perish.

Eventually my parents too began discussing the possibility of our moving to the Russian part of Poland, which included Kovel, where my mother's oldest sister lived. My aunt had reported that she and her family were suffering no hardships, and urged us to join them. My mother favored the move, my father did not. As a compromise they decided that he should go to Kovel alone, and if he found that conditions were in fact better there he would send for us.

During my father's absence my mother took charge of the candle factory. She was no stranger to the business, the employees were loyal, and there were friends and relatives whom she could call on for advice if she needed it. For about a month after my father's departure all went well. Then one morning, after she had left for the factory as usual, two Jewish men carried my mother back into our apartment. She was so disfigured as to be almost unrecognizable. Her face was battered and swollen, she had lost two teeth, and her nose, her beautiful nose, was broken.

She could hardly talk, and yet she kept repeating, "Don't worry, it is not so bad. It does not hurt so much." For the first time I saw for myself what the Nazis were capable of doing. Just looking at my mother filled me with terror and grief, with a helpless rage more wracking than anything I had ever felt before. Later, learning the details only added to my fury and bewilderment.

When my mother arrived at the factory that morning she found the door locked, with an official paper posted on it stating that this place must remain closed until further notice. She knew the order had to be obeyed, but she also knew that one of the men on the night shift was trapped inside. He had to be saved, and because at that moment no one was around she removed the notice, unlocked the door, and released the laborer. She had relocked the door and was about to replace the notice when a member of the Gestapo appeared.

Without a word he began to hit her savagely all over her body, but with particular attention to her face. She knew better than to offer resistance and kept as still as possible. Her chief concern was that the attacker might fracture her skull, so she kept her hands over her head. It was a wonder that her fingers, though hideously bruised and swollen, were not broken. When she finally fell, unable to move, the German left. Behind shut doors and windows there had been witnesses to the episode but they had known that attempts to interfere would be fatal. Now two came out, helped my mother into a carriage, and accompanied her home.

The healing process was protracted and painful. For many days my mother could barely move. She never complained, and her stoic attitude deepened my solicitude for her. Then, quite as arbitrarily as they had locked it up, the Nazis reopened the factory and my mother was again in charge, just as if there had been no interruption.

Not long afterward my father returned from Kovel. He had gone reluctantly, and what he had seen of Russian Poland had done little to change his views. To my mother's insistent questions he replied that the Russians were quite as repressive and arbitrary as the Germans. "There is no respect for the individual, none whatsoever," he told her. Then, with bitter humor, he said, "In Russia there are three categories of citizens—those who were in prison, those who are in prison, and those who will be in prison."

Within a few months, however, events would force him to concede that he had made a terrible mistake and that we really would have been better off under the Russians. But by then it was too late. The border between the two Polands was sealed. We were trapped.

Shortly after their arrival, the Nazis took over all large Jewish businesses including our chemical factory. As director of ours and one other chemical factory, they installed a man who belonged to the German minority which lived in Poland and which chose to identify with the occupier. They became a privileged group: the *Volksdeutscher*. This man, now called commissioner, moved from the position of an obscure administrator to one of prominence. After he took over, all Jewish owners were allowed to stay on as laborers. Since employment in the factory was not compulsory, my father decided against it, saying, "As long as I don't have to, I will not work for the Germans." And even though he did not work there, he was given working papers along with the others.

Protected by these papers, my father devoted all his energies to the running of the candle factory, which was bringing in considerable profits.

The Germans could do almost anything they wanted, and they often entered homes without warning—particularly Jewish homes—and helped themselves to anything they chose. People hid what they could, but it was not possible to hide furniture. We had several pieces of furniture with a shiny honey-gold finish. After considerable debate, we covered it with a special black paint that was guaranteed removable; when Poland's ordeal ended, the furniture would be as good as new.

One Nazi restriction followed another, and soon our part of the city was declared *Judenrein,* which meant that Jews could neither live in nor visit this section of Lublin. The order specified that not more than one room should be allotted to a Jewish family.

We had to find a place in a less desirable part of town. We took the news calmly, accepting my father's position that one cried for people, not for things.

A friend of ours lived close to the old city in an apartment consisting of three rooms and a kitchen, and he offered one to us. Into this room we moved what we could of our once-beautiful but now blackened furniture: a wardrobe, a table with four chairs, and two beds, one for my parents, and one for my sister and me.

Here, as in most houses, each room was heated by a separate stove built into the wall. The bottom of this stove had a small door with an opening in which was placed either coal or wood. Above this door was another with a small enclosure that served as a combination stove and burner. Soon after we had moved in, a third family arrived to share the apartment, which put a considerable strain on the kitchen. Although none of us were Orthodox, the pork products my father enjoyed might have offended some of the others, so in cold weather when the windows were closed we fried bacon and ham in our room.

Once, as we were sitting around the table waiting for our bacon to be done, there was a knock at the door. An old, bearded, highly respected man had come to ask my father to mediate a dispute between two Jews who had promised to abide by father's verdict. The matter had to be explained in detail, and as the story began to unfold, so did the smell of frying bacon, until it permeated the whole room. My eyes were glued to the stove, but our pious elderly visitor was either tactful or not alert. The visit took what seemed an eternity. And by the time the man finally took his departure, the shriveled black nubbins left in the pan bore little resemblance to bacon.

Even though food was becoming scarce, much of our time was spent in the kitchen. With three women preparing meals and all the children on hand, it was a lively place. I liked housework, and was happy to be of help. Besides, I found the talk that went on there exciting. Rumors found their way first into the kitchen, and were shared later with the others. In the evenings, when all the chores were done, adults congregated in the kitchen to discuss the current situation and speculate about the future. These conversations were predominantly somber—the present was grim enough, and everyone knew the future might well be worse.

A curfew was now in effect for Jews, and they had to be off the streets by eight o'clock. No one dared disobey. People were shot on sight for the smallest transgression, and we children were discouraged from roaming around outside even during the day.

Another rule required Jews to sew a yellow Jewish star on their clothes. Noncompliance met with a severe beating, even with death. My father hated the idea, but he was no fool and was not about to risk his life. Because of his blue eyes, and blond hair, it probably would not have occurred to the Germans that he was Jewish, but there was always the risk that some Pole he knew might denounce him. Reluctantly he agreed to my mother's sewing stars on his clothes. Even more than the star, he hated the further requirement that every Jewish man must bow low and remove his hat when he encountered a German. My father worked out a system that kept him from having to comply. Whenever he saw a German approaching, he would quickly enter a courtyard and stay there until the German had passed by. We children proudly approved of my father's system, but my mother was very upset. "What if one of the soldiers notices? Do you want to die a hero?" She would beg and cry, to no avail.

I soon realized how fortunate my father was. One day, as I stood near a window overlooking our courtyard, I heard loud screaming and shouting. Then I saw an old bearded Jew being dragged in through the gate by two German soldiers. His black caftan was in disarray, his hat was gone, and his hair was terribly dishevelled. His attackers yelled at him contemptuously, and shoved him against a wall, where they kept him in a half-leaning, half-standing position while they hit him indiscriminately on the head, shoulders, chest, and stomach. He did not defend himself. I only heard him plead, "Oh my God, oh my God."

His voice became steadily weaker, blood gushed down his face. Then he slipped down and fell away from the wall. When the soldiers tried to prop him up he fell again. He made no sound at all. The soldiers kicked him again and again with their meticulously polished boots, but he continued to lie motionless. They finally stopped, shrugged their shoulders, and left.

Close to the window, paralyzed with horror, I continued to watch. Soon a door on the ground floor opened. Two people emerged. Cautiously and slowly they looked around. Then, quickly, they lifted what looked to me like a dead man, and carried him inside their house.

I could not talk about this incident to anyone, not even to my parents. For days the old man's cries rang inside my head, and the pleading "Oh my God, oh my God" stayed with me a long time. Even though

I had lived under the Nazis for over a year this was the most direct encounter I had yet had with the reality of the occupation.

Little did I know that by comparison with later events, this reality would lose its shattering impact. Nor did I know that by November, 1942, a train would be taking me to Warsaw, into an unknown Christian world.

CHAPTER THREE

———◆▶———

The Search Begins

THE TRAIN was slowing down. The locomotive made unhappy and complaining noises. "Finally, Warsaw," I heard a weary voice say.

The exhausted, drowsy passengers began to stir, lift luggage down from the rack, put on coats, comb their hair. The optimists among them tried unsuccessfully to remove the wrinkles from their clothes with the palms of their hands. All this went on in silence and in partial darkness.

It was a gloomy autumn morning. Through the dirty wet windows a gray light tried to penetrate into our crowded compartment. Only then could I make out the faces of the passengers. As I watched them I began to wonder how many were Jewish. "Surely we are not the only ones," I thought. Indeed, whenever I heard about Jews who wanted to pass, they were all going to Warsaw. Warsaw was a big city. In Warsaw Jews could become lost in a crowd and never be recognized. "If Jews come here it must be safe!" I was glad to know that we had arrived in such a safe place.

As the train came to a full stop I moved closer to my mother. Without quite knowing why I felt a sensation of fear. This time even my mother's closeness helped little. Already eleven, I knew that I had to appear calm by substituting numbness for this fear.

Outside the train a dark, cold, drizzly morning greeted us. Passively, almost noiselessly, passengers left the train. Then I noticed German gendarmerie scattered all over the platform, and an involuntary shudder went through me, followed by an added pressure from my mother's hand. I welcomed her closeness. Now it gave me courage.

As more passengers continued to fill the platform, the Nazis quickly and decisively began to circulate among them. Here and there a German was accompanied by a Polish youth. Then I heard the familiar *"Jude, Jude."* With flashlights they illuminated faces. The people they selected were roughly pushed in the direction of a nearby building.

And as more passengers kept reaching the platform, the Nazis and their helpers began to move faster and faster. It was as if they were in a terrible hurry, almost in a frenzy. The use of flashlights increased as they kept illuminating the eyes. Jews had sad eyes. We knew that Jews could be recognized by the sadness of their eyes. It was well known. Already in Lublin my parents had kept telling me, "Pretend you are happy. Think about happy things. You must try to have happy eyes! No sad eyes."

With an assumed indifference I discreetly watched the frantic movements of the Gestapo and listened to their *"Jude, Jude."* I wondered why this was happening here. Warsaw was supposed to be safe. How did the Nazis know that so many Jews were coming here?

We moved slowly toward the gate together with the crowd. My father stayed close behind us. I pretended not to see the widely circulating Gestapo. When my mother held out our papers, the Nazi at the gate barely glanced at them. He smiled at me and patted my blond hair. Out of the corner of my eyes I could see that my father passed the inspection.

Boldly and decisively he hailed a carriage, and soon we were moving toward Bolek's place.

The three of us felt much but said nothing. I was unaware of the streets we moved along, the buildings we passed, too engrossed in myself to notice what I later learned was a beautiful section of the city.

When we reached the house where Bolek lived, we announced ourselves, as was customary, to the janitor. She was a big, fat woman. She directed us to Bolek's apartment with a knowing, familiar smile, and a wink. None of us acknowledged the smile. I resented her, wondering if she could possibly know who we were. Later I found out that she did indeed know who Bolek and his guests were, and that she was paid generously for her cooperation.

A sleepy woman opened the apartment door. "Jewish" crossed my mind. Without a question she led us into a spacious room, and disappeared.

For the first time in many hours I could see my parents' faces more clearly. The wrinkles on my father's forehead told me how tense he was, and my mother looked exhausted. Anxiously I listened to the sounds of a waking household. Then the door opened and my sister burst into the room. She was hugging and kissing us, bubbling over with happiness and excitement. Then with a big smile and outstretched arms Bolek rushed in. He hugged each of my parents, and said ebulliently, "For me this is a great day! To have you as my guests is marvelous. Well, well. . . ."

Still talking away, he lifted me up and planted a kiss on both my cheeks. He threw me in the air: "Oh, you are a pretty *shiksaleh*, you are!" I did not mind. I was grateful for his warm welcome and could see that my parents were, too. As happy to see us as my sister was, he kept talking and beaming, insisting that from now on we would have nothing to worry

about. It was clear that he believed his own pro-
nouncements.

By degrees, with my sister as official guide and
teacher, I began to take in our new surroundings.
The apartment had six rooms, one of which we were
all to share. The rooms were spacious, all richly and
elegantly decorated, with many oriental rugs and
much mahogany, crystal, and silver.

My sister introduced me to a most attractive young
woman who she later told me was Bolek's mistress.
She was clearly someone of breeding. She had lost
her family and depended entirely on our cousin. He
doted on her, calling her his pigeon, but it was hard
to know how she felt about him. In public she never
showed him any affection, and this irritated me. I
wanted her to love him as much as he loved her, and
to be as demonstrative.

Among Bolek's other guests was a middle-aged
couple, now penniless, whom he had taken in because he felt sorry for them. To repay him they tried
to keep the place in top condition, and spent most of
their time cleaning and cooking. There were also
two young men, brothers, who were about to go to a
farm outside the city, where they hoped to remain for
the duration of the war, passing as Polish farmhands.

Bolek's household bustled with life and activity. It
was a combination clearing center and shelter. People
were constantly coming and going. Some stayed only
a few hours, some several days. Most of them were
Jews, but there were also Poles and Germans, and
whoever came was welcome. Bolek provided food
for everybody. Part of his business had to do with
the buying and selling, and possibly the manufacture
of false documents, which he gave free of charge to
those who could not pay. He also arranged hiding
places for escaping Jews, and again did not insist on
payment. He was a truly generous and kind man,
who took satisfaction in doing good for people. At
Bolek's suggestion, my sister and I exchanged our

false birth certificates for new ones, which were duplicates of real documents. We were now officially sisters. I became Christina and she Danuta Bloch. The diminutive of Christina was Krysia, of Danuta was Danka, and from then on everybody had to address us by these names. Even when we were alone with our parents, we were Christina or Krysia, Danuta or Danka, and no other names could be used. This rule was followed by every Jew who had Polish identification papers.

Learning our new names was only an easy first step. We also had to learn the names of our "new" father and mother, and their ages and birthplaces as well as our own. The rest of the information, such as our mother's maiden name, father's occupation, the existence of siblings and grandparents and much more, we had to invent.

As we wove the stories of our new lives we had to be consistent. Because we were sisters, the "facts" had to match perfectly. To simplify matters some of our relatives were "dead." But too much death in one family could also arouse suspicion. These were all important considerations that had to be worked out with care.

Also essential was familiarity with the Catholic religion, its tenets and rituals. To remain a stranger to Catholicism was dangerous. Stories circulated about Jews who lost their lives because of religious ignorance. All of us—the entire household—were eager to learn. We memorized prayers and tested each other over and over again. Whenever we had a problem our Christian visitors would explain and help. There was a lot to learn, but we had time. Unless we had to, we never left the apartment.

Bolek was the only one who could and did move freely about the city. His was a privileged position. Many Germans and Poles knew who he was and knew that he lived in a section of Warsaw already off limits to Jews, and yet nothing happened to him.

We did not understand why he and his household enjoyed this extraordinary protection. Clearly, his false-paper business could not account for the protection he enjoyed, nor for his wealth.

In the privacy of our room my mother would again and again raise the same questions. What did Bolek do for the Nazis in exchange for all this? My father refused to speculate, and was annoyed when any of us let our imagination roam. Too much fantasy might be dangerous, he warned us. We didn't need to know. Despite this, he made no secret of his unhappiness with our situation. He considered any association with the Nazis distasteful, shortsighted, and dangerous. Many people were passing through Bolek's household; any of the Jews who left might fall into the hands of the Nazis. The possibility was real that when questioned and under duress, they would reveal everything. And who knew if Bolek's protection would then be powerful enough to extend to those still taking refuge with him?

With mounting urgency, our parents discussed with my sister and me the need to move on. I had to revise my first belief about Warsaw. The city was unsafe precisely because it was a center for runaway Jews.

Here as elsewhere in their efforts to apprehend Jews, the Nazis received the help of Polish collaborators. As a rule they were marginal characters who were also blackmailers. On their own, threatening exposure, they extorted money from Jews until there was no more to extort. Then they would often deliver their victims to the Gestapo. Poles could identify a Jew more easily than Germans, so those of us who lived on the Aryan side feared them more than we feared the Germans. We had no way of knowing whether a given Pole was a foe or friend. Still, we knew that there were Christian Poles who were protecting Jews. After all, without the help of Poles we would never have escaped from Lublin, and our decision to do so had been based on the conviction that somehow we would find Christians who would give us shelter and protection.

Although Bolek would be genuinely sorry to see us go, he had been trying to find such Poles for us. Before long he located a couple, Jan and Magda; despite the tremendous risk, and for a handsome sum of money, they were willing to have us share their apartment. Childless and alone, they lived in a workingclass neighborhood on the outskirts of Warsaw. Jan was an unskilled laborer with only occasional employment. No one ever came to visit him and Magda, which in itself was an advantage. But there was also a serious drawback to this proposed new setup—no hiding place could be built in the apartment that would give us protection against Nazi searches. Yet my parents were convinced that it would, at least temporarily, be safer than Bolek's, and so we moved there.

The new apartment consisted of two rooms and a kitchen. It was cluttered with oversized furniture, which Magda dusted and polished from morning to night. She also talked from morning to night, without waiting for anyone to answer. Jan, on the other hand, was a vigorous and handsome man, genial on the surface, but—as we soon learned—with a violent temper when he was sufficiently goaded. And Magda seemed to take a perverse pleasure in goading him. She would begin by complaining that he was lazy, that he didn't really want to work, so that if it were not for us, he and she would surely starve to death; and then she would go on to accuse him of running after other women. At first Jan would listen impassively, and as Magda's fervor mounted he would urge her, still with apparent calm, to stop. But Magda could not stop—compulsive in everything she did, she would rant on until she touched off his suppressed fury. And then he would start hitting her, pounding her with his big fists until her tirades gave way to tears. She wept frequently, and her face was rarely without a bruise of some sort. Yet she seemed unable to control herself. A day or so after one quarrel had ended, she would initiate another, all without any obvious provocation.

During these scenes we stayed in our room, pretending to ignore what was happening. I found Magda and Jan's relationship very strange and I kept wondering why they stayed together. Only my sister gave me an answer, and all she said, though she said it knowingly, was, "This is how such people live."

On the flat roof of the house, Jan had built a large cage, in which he kept chickens and a rooster. We ate some of the eggs, but he put others aside for hatching, and when the chicks grew to respectable size he would sell them. He would never kill any of the chickens himself. In fact, he was unusually gentle with them. He often referred to them as "ladies" and had a special name for each one. He made me feel that they were almost human.

One evening when we were all lingering around the table, Jan was talking about his "ladies," as he so often did. My parents listened politely and nodded. Then I heard myself say, "You seem to love your chickens more than your wife. Maybe they are the mistresses she complains about?" I could not understand why no one laughed. In the dead silence my father's eyes seemed to pierce mine, but nobody else looked at me at all, or at one another. Later my sister told me that in the future I had better stay away from jokes. I made up my mind that I would.

Of the four of us only my father officially lived in the apartment, and he served as our contact with the outside world. Through him we kept hearing about people disappearing. Denunciations were the order of the day. Almost without exception they had tragic consequences.

One day my father came home with news about his former partner, Mr. Lerner. Like us, he and his daughter and son-in-law had been hiding with a Polish family in Warsaw. One evening their landlady burst into the apartment crying that the Gestapo was in the courtyard, and soon they heard footsteps on the stairs and German voices approaching. They were convinced that someone had denounced them and it was too late to hide or escape. Mr. Lerner was a proud man, determined never to be taken alive, and for just such an eventuality as this one he always carried poison with him. He swallowed it. But the Gestapo never came in. They were looking for someone else in a different building, and had entered this one by mistake.

Mr. Lerner died, and his daughter and son-in-law confronted an ordeal. The responsibility for disposing of the dead body was theirs alone. They decided the only recourse was to cut it into manageable parts, each of which they wrapped in a separate package; late at night the son-in-law clandestinely threw them one by one into the river. Long afterward, the daughter and son-in-law were denounced themselves, but Mr. Lerner was not there to face it.

Our close confinement, our uncertainty about the future, the constant threat that hung over us—all these were taking their toll. I worried most about my mother, and tried to hide my own misery. She who had been so talkative and lively in the past became unusually quiet and subdued. She behaved as if she had lost some of her will to live. More than ever, she passively followed any of my father's suggestions.

My sister also changed. By now she was fifteen. She had always seemed more mature than most girls her age, but here in Warsaw she appeared almost totally adult. At the same time, she was losing her self-assurance, was becoming passive like my mother. And, like my mother, she seemed more willing to listen, less eager to advise.

For answers and explanations all three of us looked to my father. He had always behaved in a restrained,

unemotional, and dignified way. Here too his out-
ward manner changed little. And yet, on closer
inspection, I noticed that the lines on his forehead
were deeper, that his steel-blue eyes had an oddly
distant and absorbed look, and that his thick eyebrows were pulled closer together. He was clearly
preoccupied and I could easily imagine why, but I
could not guess at his innermost thoughts. He never
revealed them to me. I wondered, often, if he had
any doubts. If so, he was careful not to show them.
On the contrary, he tried to give us courage by
insisting that eventually we would overcome our difficulties and all would be well. He wanted us to
believe him, and we did. He wanted us to lean on
him, and we did. And as he was giving us support,
he also kept us informed about his efforts to find a
solution for our problems.

He was systematic in this as in everything else.
Every day he would meet with various people, ask
for suggestions, follow leads, and then start over
again, always with extreme patience and self-control.
Of course he was not alone in his search. Other Jews
too were persistently looking for new ways to survive. Their efforts gave rise to a variety of schemes,
some of which, conceived in desperation, were impossible at the outset. Others could and should have
succeeded, but ended in disaster.

One day father told us that Jews were buying
illegal passage to Hungary, where Jews lived in peace,
and that he had met a Jewish man who could arrange for us to be smuggled across the Hungarian
border. This seemed like an opportunity too good to
be missed, and despite the money involved we decided to take advantage of it. Shortly after we delivered the money the man in question disappeared.
We never knew whether he was a crook or simply
one more unfortunate Jew who had perished.

Later on help came through my father's friend
Zygmunt Rubin. He was the son of a rich brewery

owner in Lublin, whom we had met again in Warsaw. He was handsome in an unusual, imposing way,
with a strongly magnetic quality, and it would have
been difficult not to notice him. Fortunately, he looked
and behaved like a Christian, so there was little danger
in his being so conspicuous. Zygmunt was in his late
twenties, and had arrived in Warsaw with his mother
and two younger brothers, Pawel, twenty-four, and
Stefan, twenty-one. At the beginning of the war his
father had had the misfortune of being ill at the time
of a Nazi raid. He was taken out of bed and shot.

Mrs. Rubin and her three sons came to Warsaw a
few days before we did. They too were trying to pass
as Poles by acquiring false papers. Although Zygmunt
and Pawel could both easily pass for Christians, Stefan
and his mother could not. Both had what was considered a "typically Jewish look." Also, like my parents, Mrs. Rubin spoke Polish poorly.

When we met Zygmunt, and later Pawel, Mrs.
Rubin and Stefan were living with a Polish family in
Otwock, a nearby town. Both remained entirely indoors; except for their well-paid hosts, no one knew
of their existence.

The two older brothers saw no reason to go into
seclusion. Besides, Zygmunt had a girlfriend who
wanted to stay in Warsaw, and he wanted to be near
her. She was Jewish and from Lublin as well, the only
survivor of a wealthy family. She was attractive,
easygoing, and spoiled, and I liked her. My father,
however, did not, and I heard him tell my mother
that she was too careless to survive, and that she
might also destroy Zygmunt.

It was through Zygmunt that we met Antek, a
Polish youth not yet twenty, a son of the family with
whom Mrs. Rubin and Stefan were staying. Antek
was a simple, pleasant young man, with a cheerful
disposition and a positive attitude toward life. Two
of his sisters were married, and Martha, the elder,
lived in Otwock. Antek told my father, that for

payment, Marta and her husband Tosiek would be willing to have my sister and me live with them. We were to pass as Marta's nieces, orphaned early in the war and now come to stay with her and Tosiek. They would tell the same story to their children, six-year-old Jurek and four-year-old Ania. My sister and I would be able to move freely about Otwock.

My parents saw this as the best opportunity that had yet presented itself, and the arrangements were completed. My father would be able to visit us on weekends, but for my mother it would be too risky to travel. When the time came to say good-bye, our hearts were heavy. We knew that we might never see our mother again, and gloomy thoughts kept coming to my mind as I tried to give her yet another hug, another kiss. My sister and I could not help weeping, but even though tears kept running down her own cheeks, my mother repeated over and over, "I am happy about this. This is our lucky chance." I wanted to tell her how much I loved her, how sorry I was that I had ever caused her trouble. Words refused to come out. And when I tried to smile through my tears, I could not.

"Oh, God," I thought, "let me see her again. I will be so good if you let me!" Then I heard father say calmly: "You must go now." With a quick embrace he pushed us out. Antek was waiting to take us to Otwock.

In Warsaw, more than ever before, I realized how important time could be. A day, an hour, even a few minutes could make a difference between life and death. Having a safe place for one night, arriving half an hour after the Gestapo left, entering an apartment under Nazi observation—any of these things took up little time, any of them could be fateful. We were never sure what time would bring next, and yet we wanted it to pass swiftly. But time moved slowly, and a day spent searching for a safe place to sleep could feel like a year. And as the difficulties and dangers kept mounting, time seemed to stand still. It refused to move on.

I had stayed in Warsaw only a few weeks. It felt like eternity.

Otwock was no more than a half hour train ride from Warsaw, but it had the rustic look and tranquil atmosphere of a small remote village. It was quite literally a town inside a forest. Except for a few commercial buildings near the railroad station, it consisted of one-story wooden structures scattered along unpaved roads that wound among tall pine trees. Through all the hours of sunlight the trees cast a shifting, flickering, mysterious pattern of shadows. Their discarded needles covered the ground like a thick, soft carpet. A strong pine aroma floated in the air. From the moment I arrived I felt there was something dreamlike about this town of modest rustic dwellings, majestic trees, and bracing air. It was the quality of Otwock's air that had made it a center for tuberculosis patients.

Many Jews had once lived there, yet we passed a number of picturesque little churches, without seeing even one synagogue. For us the fate of Otwock's Jews had to remain a forbidden subject. Even to refer to it might be disastrous.

The house to which Antek took us resembled most of the others. It was a one-story wooden structure, with a porch on all four sides. When we came close I noticed peeling paint, a broken step, and a partly rotten porch railing. Half the house was occupied by a middle-aged woman and her niece, half by Marta and her family. This half consisted of a kitchen and a single large room that was the center of all activity. In one corner was a cast-iron stove, which served both for heating and for cooking. Right next to it stood a large wardrobe, and in each of the other three corners was a bed. A large rectangular table surrounded by wooden chairs filled the center of the room, and a bare bulb hanging over it provided the only light.

Marta greeted us without so much as a smile and without bothering to introduce us to Jurek and Ania, who were hiding behind the wardrobe. She was a tall woman with large bones, an imposing figure, and brown short hair that had been treated to an imperfect permanent. Behind her heavy-rimmed glasses, I saw lively and intelligent brown eyes. Her features were sharp—a thin nose, thin lips, a triangular chin. Her skin was smooth but pale. Her size, her glasses, her sharp features, her pallor, combined to make her somewhat forbidding. She conveyed the impression of an intelligent woman who was also cold and unapproachable. I noticed that Antek had become unusually quiet in his sister's presence, and he left sooner than I expected or wanted him to.

In her stern, unsmiling way, Marta explained that two people would sleep in each bed: she and her husband, Jurek and Ania, my sister and I. "When your father visits you, we will arrange a bed on the floor near the stove," she told us. "We eat dinner at eight, after my husband comes home. And now," she said, "you are free to do whatever you want."

We went for a walk. It was a relief for us to be alone together. We moved slowly through the dreamlike quiet and the shimmering shadows under the towering pines, and we agreed that this was a safe place and that we were fortunate to be here. The rest was unimportant.

When we returned, Jurek and Ania did approach us, though shyly and hesitantly. But as soon as their father arrived they underwent a transformation. They became wild with joy, shouting, jumping, hurling themselves against him. To all this he responded with bear hugs and kisses. Still smiling, he turned from his children to us, saying: "Welcome, welcome! Feel at home, you must feel at home here!"

I liked him right away. Physically as well as in

manner Tosiek was totally different from Marta. He was a small, slight man, a few inches more than five feet, with regular delicate features, merry dark eyes and black hair that was glued to his skull with some scented lotion. In no time we discovered that he had an easygoing cheerful disposition and seemed always ready with a joke.

We also learned that Tosiek's father had been an unskilled laborer and that he had died when Tosiek was barely into his teens. This sent Tosiek to work, and forced his mother to become a cleaning woman. His present job was a manual one in a Warsaw movie house, having to do with projectors, and he worked long hours. Traveling to and from the city to work, he was away from home for fourteen hours or more every day.

It was clear that Marta enjoyed harping on her husband's humble parentage and present menial employment. She came from a more "distinguished" family. Her father, Stanislaw, had been a nobleman, a fact that neither he nor she would let anyone forget. During World War I, as an officer in the Polish army, he had been severely wounded, and in the hospital he was given large dosages of morphine to alleviate his suffering. He became an addict, and never fully recovered from either his addiction or his injuries. He went from the military hospital to his older brother's house, where he stayed for a year. During that time Maria, a maid who worked in the household, had the responsibility of caring for him. She dressed his wounds, fed him, and attended to all his other needs uncomplainingly.

Maria was a young, soft-spoken, simple girl, devoted to her task and to her patient, and as Stanislaw began to feel better he realized that he could not do without her. They married. Because of her position and her background this was an excellent match for her, but for Stanislaw it was a social comedown—a fact that he never let Maria forget.

Of their three children, Martha was the least attractive and the most intelligent and studious. She became a schoolteacher, which entitled her to some social recognition. But she practiced her profession for only a short time, because she developed tuberculosis. She spent a year in a sanitarium, and after that was ordered to lead as restful a life as possible, in a healthful environment. It was in fact Martha's illness that had brought the whole family to Otwock, for the sake of the bracing air. Eventually her illness was arrested but she was never completely well, and her doctor warned her that she could have a relapse at any time.

Plain and in poor health, Martha did not have good prospects for finding a husband, and she should have been grateful that a man as kind, relaxed, and personable as Tosiek had wanted to marry her. Instead she felt that she, in turn, had married beneath her own class.

Without mutual warmth and affection, their marriage soon became difficult, full of conflicts and quarrels. Easygoing and amiable though he was, Tosiek eventually rebelled. When Martha was pregnant with their second child, he left her. Martha put aside her social pretensions and begged him to return. After a year's absence, Tosiek returned to her. From then on, whenever they had a serious quarrel Martha would acquiesce. She was no fool, and she had learned her lesson. Tosiek could always leave her again.

Martha's parents and the Rubins lived nearby, in an equally modest house that was also in need of repairs. The rough wooden floors were bare, the furniture was rickety, and the windows were small and uncurtained. But this house had two rooms in addition to the kitchen. The kitchen was the most spacious and therefore used as the all-purpose daytime living room. Antek even slept there. Maria and Stanislaw slept in the larger of the other two rooms. The third was modest indeed, with only one small window close to the ceiling, and for all practical purposes might not have been part of the house at all. From the outside one could not have guessed its existence and on the inside it could easily be camouflaged. A massive heavy wardrobe had been placed in front of the door, and the room could be entered only after one removed a special board, itself well camouflaged in the wardrobe's back wall.

This was the room in which Stefan and his mother lived. It was furnished with two iron beds, a stove, a table, and two chairs. A pail standing in a curtained-off corner served as a toilet. Maria supplied water, fuel, and food, and Mrs. Rubin prepared all the meals for herself and Stefan. This was her main occupation, which helped her pass the otherwise empty, monotonous hours. No one outside the family knew of the Rubins's existence. They left the room only on rare occasions, and when they did it was always after dark.

Even before I met him I had heard that Stefan would be unattractive. But when I actually faced him, his ugliness surpassed my expectations. His nose was so prominent, his lips were so thick, his eyebrows were so unusually bushy, that at first I hardly noticed how intelligent his eyes were. Although he was of medium height he had a bad stoop, and he appeared almost dwarfish. I wondered if he kept his head down between his shoulders to hide his ugly face.

When he turned to me in a friendly way, greeting me not like a child but like an equal, I felt uneasy, and as he tried to explain to me in a half-mocking half-serious way what a paradise Otwock was, my aversion gave way to pity. "It must be terrible," I thought, "to be so ugly and have such handsome brothers!"

I wanted to do something to ease his burden, and I discovered that this would not, after all, be too difficult. What Stefan lacked in looks he made up for with a sparkling personality. Despite the conditions he now lived under he never lost his sense of humor. Instead of complaining he made fun of his circumstances, often laughing at himself and at his inability to move freely. His observations about everyday occurrences were original and amusing, and he was full of humorous stories and songs, some of which he made up as he went along. He made a fine friend. He was fun to be with. And yet, underneath his almost buoyant surface, I sensed a certain inevitable bitterness.

It was obvious that neither his wit nor his intelligence came from Mrs. Rubin, who was quiet, limited, and dull. She could not qualify as a companion for her bright son, so it was not surprising that almost any visitor delighted him. My sister and I enjoyed him and the special welcome he gave us. We also enjoyed the stories he shared with us about Marta and her family.

It was he who told us that Stanislaw, because of his injuries, had never held a job. Still, the fact that Stanislaw was unemployed did not mean he was idle. He was endlessly busy—busy with his poppy seeds. In the back, at the edge of his property, was the customary outhouse. The land between the house and the outhouse was given to the cultivation of poppies. He used poppy seeds to gratify his need for narcotics, and he insisted that he could not live without them.

Before he could brew his tea from the poppy seeds he had to work hard. First he had to fertilize the soil, then he had to plant the poppy seeds. He had to tend and weed and water the crop; when it ripened he had to cut the poppies and make sure that they dried evenly, at the proper temperature. This, too, required constant attention. Later he subdivided the seed heads into separate piles, which had to dry further behind the stove in the kitchen. The end product was a tea that he claimed had the same effect as opium. He referred to it as his medication, insisting that without it he could not survive the pain. He never increased the amount he used. He was an addict, but kept his addiction within bounds.

Stanislaw was selfish and wholly self-centered. He focused his whole attention on his own suffering and on growing poppies to relieve it. He expected others to do the same. He was also grumpy. Yet his self-absorption and his grumpiness were oddly inoffensive. Not only did he insist that he was very sick, but also that he was blind. But how could a blind man attend to the cultivation of poppies and the brewing of tea? Why would a blind man, stroking my hair, call me his "golden one"? I remember an evening when we were sitting around the table before a bowl of freshly fried potato pancakes; he turned his head to say, "Maria, hand me a pancake. I can't see where they are," and when Maria complied, he cried out, "No, no, not the burned one!"

But no one discussed these little contradictions, nor did anyone seem to object to him or his behavior.

Maria had a hard life. Besides taking care of her husband's constant demands for attention, she also ran a meat stall at the local market. After the war started this had become a black-market operation, but Maria ignored whatever danger was involved and kept on working. She was patient, submissive, undemanding, satisfied with her lot. Totally unlike Stanislaw, she never complained. Her moods showed no variations. Her entire person spelled moderation. Because of this she was a colorless person and she did not appeal to me at all.

As for Marta, closer acquaintance with her did little to change our initial negative opinion. She appeared to dislike everyone except her father and her son Jurek, toward whom she did show affection. When she spoke about her father she emphasized his intelligence and his noble birth, but her affection for Jurek was more personal. He was a thin, good-looking boy, with a pale complexion that convinced his mother he would be stricken with consumption. In anticipation of this disaster she spoiled him. According to Marta, Jurek could do no wrong, could tell no lie. In fact he was a pampered brat who knew quite well how to take advantage of his privileged situation. Especially toward his sister Ania he showed a lot of cruelty. He would pinch or hit her and then deny that he had done anything. My sister and I soon learned that even if we knew he was lying, we must not say a word. Once or twice when we tried to intervene, Marta was furious and called us liars and connivers. After that we tried to stay away from Jurek and ignored him as much as possible.

The one member of the household we really liked and enjoyed was Tosiek. But he would leave the house in the early morning to catch his train and not return until around eight in the evening. Sunday was his day off, which turned it into a happier day. He was kind to my sister and me, always making sure the two of us were included in family conversations, and he even went out of his way to entertain us with jokes and anecdotes and comic songs. With Tosiek home, even Marta was less disagreeable.

In his absence Marta was cold and sarcastic. She kept us busy with household chores and she was hard to please, invariably criticizing whatever we did. Since she was a mediocre housekeeper, her displeasure was due to maliciousness, not to her desire for orderliness and cleanliness.

The entire house had an unappealing and neglected appearance. The wooden floors were bare and of a nondescript gray, and should have been cleaned with water and a scrubbing brush. Instead, the only care they ever received was a casual sweep with a broom. The windows had neither shades nor curtains; the pine trees surrounding the house provided enough privacy. The kitchen was small and cluttered; it was the place where dishes got washed, but otherwise no more than a storage area, left unheated for economy's sake. All the cooking was done in the main room.

There was one occasion when the kitchen was heated, however. On the rare times that members of the family took a bath, the stove in the kitchen was lit and used to heat pots of water. Each of us took turns at washing in a large wooden bathtub. This was quite a procedure. We had to pour clean water in and the dirty water out, which seemed to take forever. There was always the risk of catching a cold. Because Marta was fearful that she would become ill again, we bathed only once a month. The rest of the time we had to be satisfied with washing in cold water. My sister and I, who were used to bathing more frequently, washed as often as we could. But our efforts aroused Marta's hostility. She saw it as an act of defiance and accused us of trying to appear superior. Whenever she caught us washing, even in cold water, she would comment sarcastically: "Trying to show off again? Who do you think you are? A couple of princesses?"

Gradually, inevitably, we succumbed to the family pattern, and the result was lice. Lice were not uncommon during the war, but until we came to Otwock my sister and I had escaped them. Now, just as with the rest of the family, our hair became infested. Marta and her family coped expertly, although their technique bore no relation to washing. Every two or three days, right after dinner, they would spread newspapers on the table and proceed to rake the lice out of their hair with special combs, squashing them with their fingernails as they fell on the paper. To be sure, it was only a partial remedy because it left the eggs intact no matter how many lice it removed. At first my sister and I were repulsed. But gradually we accepted it as a natural part of life. And later we even welcomed it, because it gave us much relief from the hungry lice.

*   *   *

Every week day started with Tosiek leaving for work. The rest of us would then get up and have breakfast, which consisted of imitation coffee, usually served black or with warm milk, and dark bread, which was cheaper than white and therefore considered inferior. Saccharine was used to sweeten the coffee because sugar was too expensive, and there was neither butter nor margarine, let alone jam, to spread on the bread. When my father visited us he would bring sugar or jam, and the quality of our breakfasts would improve a little. Dinner, the only other meal, was not served until Tosiek returned in the evening. As a rule it consisted of just soup, a mixture of potatoes, beans, carrots, beets, cabbage, and other vegetables, which had been put into one big black and left on the stove to simmer for hours. On rare occasions the soup just might include a little meat, or at least a few bones.

Marta and her children had grown used to this and seemed to suffer no hunger pangs between breakfast and dinner. But my sister and I felt starved. We were reluctant to ask for food, and we did not dare take it ourselves. Besides, there was not much food around. At the most one could find some bread and vegetables, which we did not feel free to touch.

My sister and I took long walks all over Otwock, and soon we knew every corner, every store and church. Sometimes we stopped in a coffee shop and treated ourselves to cakes and tea, or bought rolls at a bakery and ate them while walking. So, now and then, we could forget about feeling hungry.

We were happy at least to have each other, and we knew better than to bother my father with our problems. He had burdens enough as it was. Besides, Otwock was a safe place, and this was the most important consideration. Although my father sensed that it was depressing, he kept emphasizing its safety. He was right. Places like ours were becoming more and more difficult to find.

Protected only by his blond, blue-eyed Nordic looks, my father came to see us once a week. Actually, it was risky for him to travel. Even a routine check of papers could have had dire consequences. Any prolonged conversation in Polish could have given him away. But it was more than his appearance that protected him. He also behaved like a Christian. He moved with assurance. He did not act or look scared. On the contrary, his piercing grayish-blue eyes under bushy eyebrows had a way of intimidating people. They kept others at a distance. In those days Jews looked frightened. They walked cautiously, without self-confidence. Most of them desperately tried to become invisible. Ironically, those very efforts made them more conspicuous.

We welcomed his visits both for the pleasure they gave us and for the news they brought of our mother. Things were not going well. They had already been forced to change apartments several times, and each move increased the possibility of discovery. Warsaw was becoming steadily more dangerous, and my father was trying hard to find a place away from the capital. I was amazed that all his unsuccessful attempts did not discourage him. But he was persistent, and not about to give up.

We also came to welcome the times twice a week when Marta joined her mother at the market to sell meat, and we stayed at home to take care of Jurek and Ania. They behaved well in their mother's absence, and we enjoyed reading stories or playing with them. Despite some of the continuing drawbacks, my sister and I were keenly aware of our good fortune.

One day a relative of Marta's named Wojtek came to visit. Marta had a younger sister, Ziutka, who lived with her husband Tadek and his family in the city of Kielce. Wojtek was Tadek's brother. He was a tall nineteen-year-old youth with blond hair, watery blue eyes, and a red face. He was friendly and open, and in an ordinary sort of way he was good looking. His permanent home was in Kielce, where he lived with the rest of his family, but he was part of a crew installing telephone poles all over the country. Ostensibly he had been passing by and decided to pay a casual visit to Maria and Stanislaw, but in fact he knew from his sister-in-law Ziutka how Stanislaw and Maria had improved their economic situation by protecting Jews. Wojtek and his family barely managed to survive on the wages the Germans paid him; he had come to find out if he and his family could also profit from such an arrangement.

He was shrewd enough not to mention any of this to his Otwock relatives. Instead he approached my sister, who directed him to our father, who in turn saw in this the opportunity he had been searching for. When father came to visit us later, he had worked out a plan whereby my sister would leave for Kielce with Wojtek and investigate conditions there, and if her impressions were favorable Wojtek would go to Warsaw to fetch our parents. For the present, I was to remain with Tosiek and Marta, but if everything worked out, I would eventually join the rest of my family in Kielce.

My father explained my sister's departure to Marta by telling her that my mother was ill and in need of my sister's attention.

For me that departure left a terrible void. I missed my sister. I missed her company and her protection. I missed her optimism. To know that the proposed move to Kielce might eventually be a fortunate development for all of us did not help me in my dejection. And to make matters worse, my father had to curtail his visits to Otwock. It was becoming increasingly dangerous to travel, and the deteriorating situation in Warsaw meant that my mother's hiding place had to be changed yet again, at even greater expense. My parents and I all impatiently waited for news from my sister, and as time passed and she sent no word of any sort, our impatience turned to dread.

Tragedy came from quite a different direction. One evening when my father arrived I could see right away that something terrible had happened. Zygmunt, his best friend, had disappeared.

My father was supposed to meet Zygmunt in their usual coffee shop. They intended to take the train together. Zygmunt, who was always on time, failed to appear, and my father began to suspect the worst. A few inquiries revealed the story.

The parents of Zygmunt's girlfriend had entrusted a large part of their fortune in jewelry and gold to a reliable Pole, with the understanding that he would return it on receiving secretly coded instructions from any member of the family. Another Pole, also a former employee, knew about this arrangement. He was aware that Zygmunt's girlfriend was now the only person capable of issuing such instructions, and he came to Warsaw with the specific aim of obtaining them. He gained the girl's confidence by offering help, and then announced his willingness to serve as a messenger and bring her whatever jewelry, gold, and other valuables the first Pole was holding for her. She gave him a letter requesting that all the valuables be entrusted to him, and they agreed to meet again at a specific time in some coffee shop. On the appointed day the girl asked Zygmunt to accompany her, and when they arrived at the coffee shop the Pole was waiting for them. Within minutes the Gestapo appeared, and arrested both Zygmunt and his girlfriend. The Pole had denounced her to gain permanent possession of the valuables he had brought from Lublin. Zygmunt was a chance victim; had he not accompanied the girl he would not have been picked up. They were never heard from again.

That evening my father and I joined the Rubins in their little room. Mrs. Rubin sat silent and motionless, looking vacantly into space. Occasionally her eyes would fill and a few tears would run down her cheeks, and at such moments she seemed more aware of herself and us. Pawel and Stefan looked stunned and grieved. All of us were very quiet, mourning and sharing in much unspoken sadness.

When we left, father and I barely talked. We went to bed with a listless "good night." I could not comfort him. Knowing him so well, I knew that he could not give vent to his emotions. He had to suffer privately and alone. Preoccupied and still saying little, he left the next morning.

Two days later my father came back, to tell me there was news from my sister. What she had reported confirmed his hope that Kielce could be the answer to our problems. He and my mother would leave for Kielce with Wojtek as soon as possible. It would be safer for me not to travel with them. He hoped that we would be reunited soon. He made arrangements to send money to Tosiek and Marta through Bolek. Should something unexpected happen, I had some jewelry and gold sewn into my clothes. My father told me I should use them only if Bolek's messenger failed to appear. There would be no writing. Only through the messenger would they notify me of their arrival. I was to tell absolutely no one about this arrangement and of course I should never, under any circumstances, tell anyone that I was Jewish. He explained to Marta that he had found a new and relatively safe hiding place near Warsaw, and that he was about to join my mother and sister there. From now on he would not be able to visit me at all.

When he told me that he had to leave in the afternoon, I did not complain. I could see how hard it was for him. I knew him too well not to recognize his suffering, and I could not cause him more pain. "I will not cry," I promised myself. I wanted to tell him not to worry about me, but instead I kept looking at him intently. I wanted to memorize his features. I had no photographs of him, because photographs were too dangerous, but I felt that if I could imprint his features on my memory I could somehow keep him with me. More than anything else in the world I wanted him to stay. But I could not tell him so.

It was time to part. My father put his arms around me and squeezed me tightly. It was a desperate, painful embrace. "Remember," he whispered. "Never tell anyone where we went. And never, never, admit to anyone that you are Jewish. No matter how hard it is, you must guard these secrets. You must be strong."

I nodded. I tried to hold on to him for another moment. My whole being was filled with tears, but they stayed inside. Decisively, though tenderly, he freed himself, and before I realized what was happening he was gone. As if in a trance, I moved to the window to get a better view of him. My tears poured out freely now but silently. It was dusk. In the deserted street, among the tall and proud pines, my father looked strangely alone and small. I saw only his slightly bent back. He was moving away from me as if in a hurry. I hoped he would turn around, but he did not. I watched him until he had disappeared. I continued to stand near the window. The road was empty, so very empty. Was I waiting for a miracle that would never come?

That night I cried myself to sleep. I was alone.

CHAPTER FOUR

———◆◆———

Left Alone

WHEN my father left I felt that a part of me had left with him, never to return, that a part of me had died. Still more terrible, I felt that my family had gone from me. With loss came mourning—for my family, for the part of me that had died, for what was no more. With my mourning came apathy and depression. In time this helped me care less, helped me to bear the excruciating, almost physical pain. It eased things little to know that I had been left behind for the sake of my own safety. And even when the news came that my parents were reunited with my sister, my acute suffering only gave way to a duller chronic pain. I could not stop wondering if they would survive, if I would ever see them again. I missed them and continued to feel unprotected and afraid.

It was fortunate for me that at this particular point Marta became preoccupied with her health and chose to ignore me. I was allowed to grieve without interference, and grieve I did.

As if to ease my suffering, Tosiek became especially kind and solicitous. Without asking how I felt, he would simply say, "Don't worry, your family is well. Your father knows how to take care of things."

So I turned to him for comfort. Each day I waited patiently for Tosiek's return. I would begin to listen for the train whistle long before afternoon turned into evening. All positive things converged with his appearance: friendliness, warmth, animated talk, and even food. In the evening we could eat as much as we wanted, and even though dinner consisted only of soup, it was good to know there would be plenty of it. I always had extra helpings, sometimes two or three. Often I ate so much that I had difficulty moving away from the table. Whenever I helped myself to more, I hoped that this would prevent me from feeling hungry the next day, but the next day I was as hungry as ever. I who for most of my eleven years had been a poor eater, who had had to be coaxed into every bite, developed an enormous appetite.

With my sister's departure, food had become more of a problem for me. Alone, I had less freedom to roam the town. If I had entered a coffee shop by myself I would have been too conspicuous. People had come to recognize me, and they could have reported my visits to Marta. In time I came up with a partial solution. I decided that a church would be an ideal place for eating, because during the day in the middle of the week the churches tended to be empty. So I bought some bread, hid it in my pocket, and entered a church. After I made sure that no one was around, I ate my bread systematically, piece by piece. The chance that I would be discovered was minimal. I never had the feeling that I was doing something disrespectful. My ideas about God may have been vague, but I was convinced that he was on my side.

There were times when I had to stay at home and it was then, as if to spite me, that my stomach demanded special attention. On the whole, I managed to ignore its demands. But one day when I was particularly hungry I gave in and I helped myself to a slice of bread. The moment Marta came home she discovered my transgression. "What is the matter?" she demanded. "Don't I feed you enough? Can't you wait for meals and eat with everybody?" I was too mortified to say a word, but there was something else that bothered me. How had she known about the missing slice of bread?

I had to satisfy my curiosity, and the next time Marta was safely away I decided to investigate. I took out the bread and carefully examined it. Sure enough, close to the edge of the crust little crosses had been carved with a knife. Anyone who cut off a slice would cut off the crosses. It occurred to me that I could fool Marta by carving new little crosses after I had cut off a piece, but I dismissed the idea right away. I was too scared; it was easier to be hungry than to run the risk of a tongue-lashing from Marta.

Much more upsetting than hunger were the bad dreams that began to torment me. I knew that my parents had arrived safely in Kielce, but this knowledge was not a part of my dream world. Night after night I dreamed that I had lost my family. I would wake up in terror, crying, convinced that I had been left alone.

And as if I did not have enough troubles, I began to wet my bed. At first I hoped that no one would notice, but nothing for long escaped Marta's eagle eyes. She was outraged and contemptuous and asked me if I wasn't ashamed of myself. I was, but shame did not help me. I began trying various remedies. Just before bedtime I would visit the outhouse and pray that no accident would happen later. But prayers and wishful thinking failed to bring about the desired effect. So I decided to drink as little as possible. When that did not work I stopped drinking altogether. But even that was of no use.

Just the anticipation of wetting the bed made me very nervous. I grew steadily more afraid of Marta, who interpreted each accident as an act of hostility directed against her. She spared me no humiliation, and made a point of abusing me in front of the children. But she never mentioned my problem to Tosiek, and for that I was grateful to her. My weakness mortified me. It made me feel like a criminal and an outcast. I became sure that anybody who would know about it would, like Marta, treat me with contempt.

During her outbursts I remained quiet and stood motionless, waiting for her screaming and insults to stop. Then I would go to the outhouse and cry. But one day I lost my self-control and burst out crying right in front of her and the children. It was as if all the pent-up frustrations, all the tensions, had to come out. Nothing mattered any more and I abandoned myself to my grief, sobbing uncontrollably and gasping for breath. The children were frightened, and came over to me and tried to comfort me by gently stroking my hair.

That evening relief came from an unexpected quarter. As we were sitting down to eat Jurek said to his father, "Today Mommy screamed at Krysia so much that she almost died crying." There was silence. Then Tosiek asked, "Why do you think Mommy was so angry?" "Oh," Jurek said, "Mommy screams at Krysia all the time, but especially when she wets her bed."

I felt myself getting red and hot with shame and I thought it would be better to die than to go through this humiliation. I felt my heart pounding, wished I could evaporate into thin air.

Tosiek paled and then he started to shout at Marta. "Why don't you leave this poor child alone, you witch? Why don't you stop torturing people?" I had never seen him so angry. I began crying again, but this time my tears ran down silently. Little Ania threw her arms around me, and I felt strangely relieved. As for Marta, she uttered not a word.

Bed wetting was never mentioned again. There

was no need. It ended as mysteriously as it had begun.

Although I felt immense gratitude to Tosiek and felt a need to confide in him, I knew that I must not monopolize his time. I stayed discreetly in the background and did not speak to him about my fears or my longing for my family, or about Marta's mistreatment. I knew that if I told Tosiek about Marta it might get back to her and only complicate matters. I was convinced that if she knew I had done so she would throw me out and if that happened not even Tosiek could help me.

In my loneliness I discovered Otwock's lending library. It became one of my friends, and I soon turned into an avid reader. It was not unusual for me to read a book a day. I particularly enjoyed stories about rich and happy girls, girls who were sent away to elegant boarding schools. Through reading and daydreams I found a wonderful way of escaping into a different and more agreeable world—a fantasy world that came to include my family, a world rich with images of happy reunions and cheerful days full of love. Reading was not without a price however. "Look at her," Marta would sneer, "her nose buried in a book again." She would think up chores for me to do. But while she could interfere with my reading, she couldn't touch my daydreams.

I also continued enjoying my visits to Marta's parents and the time I spent with Stanislaw and the Rubins. Even though the secret room behind the wardrobe was a gloomy place, I felt protected there, and less tense. As my visits went on I began noticing a curious thing about the room's floor: it was unevenly clean, and the clean and dirty patches varied from one visit to the next. I discovered that Stefan was responsible for this condition. He was a great believer in systems—there had to be one for every undertaking no matter how mundane. He had volunteered to keep the floor clean, and had decided that instead of scrubbing it all at once it would be more efficient to do so in stages. He had therefore subdivided the floor into six even parts, and each day he scrubbed just one part. The result was a floor that was never wholly clean, but Stefan took great satisfaction in taking care of it systematically.

I became increasingly grateful for Stefan's friendship and increasingly impressed by his cleverness, his wit, and the wealth of information that he had acquired.

Sometimes, on moonless nights, I would offer to take the Rubins for a walk. Mrs. Rubin always refused, but for Stefan this was a special treat. Without me he would not have ventured into the street, even when it was very dark. With me he felt safe. He would tease me by saying, "Krysia, I don't need you for protection, just for your golden hair." Infrequent though they were, these walks were important for both of us. As we made our way slowly beneath the whispering pine trees, Stefan would softly sing funny songs to me, tell jokes, or speak seriously about his hopes and dreams. All of this helped me to forget my own problems, and allowed each of us to pretend that both our dreams would come true.

I also began shopping for the Rubins. They had been depending on Maria to make all their purchases, and I found out that she had been doing so at a considerable profit, sometimes charging them double. I knew that they were already paying generously for their stay in Otwock. This additional profit outraged my sense of justice. Besides, I felt that shopping for the Rubins was a way of repaying them for their kindness.

It was lucky that during our nighttime walks no curious person caught a glimpse of Stefan. If anyone had, it could have been disastrous for both of us. It was equally lucky that no one discovered that I occasionally shopped for the Rubins which, after all, deprived Maria of a profit. I did not consider the risks involved, nor was I fully aware of them, and the Rubins never chose to enlighten me about them. Our friendship remained undisturbed, and it went on playing an important part in my life.

But my pleasure in Stefan's company was marred by the fact that I could not be completely open and honest with him. I was afraid to tell him about Marta's mistreatment of me. I thought that he might repeat what I said to Marta's parents. I was convinced that if Marta heard about it she would throw me out. I had nowhere to go. I knew that friends could be of little help. I did not expect the Rubins to risk their security for me; on that score I had no illusions. I also knew that I had to be particularly guarded about my family's whereabouts and the plans for our eventual reunion. Stefan sensed that I was keeping secrets from him and suspected that my family was not quite so close to Warsaw as I had told him. He tried hard to find out the truth. At different times and in different ways he would suggest that I should have no secrets from him, that good friends had to confide in each other and that he kept no secrets from me. His remarks made me uncomfortable. Friendship did mean no secrets. I knew that.

Yet I remained silent. I could not act otherwise even though I felt like a traitor. He did not believe me, but that did not really matter. What mattered was that I could and did continue to keep my secrets.

At the Rubins' I would occasionally meet Stefan's brother Pawel. For me his visits were a welcome diversion. He was self-assured, easygoing, full of fun, and very handsome. In contrast to Stefan he treated me like a child. He would put me on his knees, pinch my cheeks, and play with me.

Stefan was far more intelligent and knowledgeable than Pawel and if I'd had to choose between them, Stefan was the brother I'd have decided on. Still, my preference did not keep me from enjoying Pawel's attentions.

We learned from Pawel that life for Jews in the capital was becoming more and more difficult. All that he told us intensified Mrs. Rubin's fears for him, and she repeatedly begged Pawel to go into hiding too. Pawel became angry whenever she broached the subject and would not hear of it. On one of my visits he blew up at her. "This is not a life!" he told her. "I could not stand this situation. You think that you are alive? You are not! You're both turning into vegetables." I was embarrassed. I wondered how he could be so brutal to his mother and brother, who had absolutely no choice. I glanced at Stefan, wondering what he would say. I knew how angry he was from a nervous twitch of his eyebrow, but he said nothing. Later when we were alone he said with a significant smile, "I trust you. I know that you know how to keep a secret." He then began to enlarge on his hatred for Pawel. He hated him for his good looks, for his independence, for his freedom, and for his lack of sensitivity. As he kept talking, his emotions seemed to carry him away, and it was as if I was not there. In the course of his long tirade Stefan called his brother a good-for-nothing brute and swore to humiliate him when the war was over. There was so much hatred in what he said that he scared me. He did not seem like my wise, kind, patient friend Stefan, but a stranger, whose anger was out of all proportion to Pawel's shortcomings.

After this episode I was more aware of the conflict between the two brothers and began noticing things I had previously overlooked. Pawel was as conceited as he was handsome, and consistently patronized Stefan. It was this patronizing attitude that infuriated Stefan the most. Still he did not directly attack Pawel. Instead, he never missed an opportunity to ridicule him, using his intellectual superiority, sometimes viciously. Often enough his sophisticated thrusts left Pawel at a loss or escaped him completely. Stefan always enjoyed the uneven battle and the victory that followed.

During our walks, Stefan would tell me, "Jews have enough enemies as it is, and it would be wrong for them to quarrel among themselves. Now more than ever we must stick together. Just wait until after the war. Then Pawel will find out which one of us is stronger."

For Pawel, though, there was no "after the war." One day, when we expected him and Antek, they did not arrive.

Now that the Germans were sending more men to the front, they had seriously depleted their civilian labor force. They were replacing German workers with able-bodied Poles rounded up in raids. As a rule, they would deport only those who could not prove they were engaged in "productive" work. Neither Antek nor Pawel had regular employment or papers that would identify them as useful workers, and thus were easy targets.

Weeks passed without any word from either of them. Eventually a letter arrived from Antek. He and Pawel had been caught in a routine roundup. They had been separated for interrogation. Antek was being transported to Germany for forced labor with all those rounded up with him. Pawel was not among them. In fact, he had not seen Pawel again. It was no longer possible to doubt that Pawel had perished.

The Rubins buried themselves in grief. They stopped eating. When I visited them they appeared oblivious to their surroundings. They behaved as if they did not care to live. Although it was no secret that Stefan had loved Zygmunt and had little affection for Pawel, he now mourned more intensely than he had for Zygmunt. It was hard for me to understand his deep depression. His suffering was manifestly real. He lost weight, he did not wash or shave, and he had withdrawn into an almost total silence. It looked as though no one could shake him out of his depression and I wondered if people really could die of grief.

Mrs. Rubin came to the rescue. One day she simply announced, "We must live. We have to remember him, just as we have to remember the others. We must not let our pain destroy us." After that we both tried to coax Stefan into eating. The process was slow, but when he returned to his system of washing a sixth of the floor each day, I knew that he was on the mend.

It soon became clear, in fact, that Pawel's disappearance had brought about a change for the positive in Stefan. He was now the official head of the family, and he acted accordingly. He obviously liked being in charge, and although this delighted me it also made me a little uncomfortable. I was sorry that I knew so much about Stefan's hatred for his brother. From then on, we never mentioned Pawel to each other.

This was the beginning of 1943, and once again time seemed to have slowed almost to a stop. I wanted time to be my servant, to obey me when I ordered it to move fast and to sweep me on to a reunion with my family. But time was my antagonist, and the unchanging present became always harder to bear. The temptation to escape from a sense of total isolation by pouring out all my secrets became so powerful that I was afraid I might yield to it. Maybe, after all, it was a good thing that time stood still.

Then, one day, something did happen. It involved the two women who shared the other half of the house. The older one, the aunt, was unattractive, with a tense inquisitive look that made me wary of her. The niece, though, had a friendly smile; she was a pretty twenty-year-old and, like her aunt, she bleached her hair.

The aunt kept house and the niece worked in a canteen for German officers, with whom she was on the most friendly terms. One or another of them came regularly to take her out on a date and brought her home late at night, making enough noise about it to disturb our sleep. None of us dared to complain. We limited our contacts with these women to an exchange of polite greetings. Because of their German connection, I took special care to stay away from them.

But soon after my father left for Kielce, the older woman began making overtures to me. When we met she would ask where I was going and how I was. Usually I tried to avoid her without appearing to be rude, because although I did not want to have anything to do with her, I did not want to offend her either. Nonetheless our meetings kept occurring more frequently, and my suspicion that she had begun deliberately following me was confirmed one day when I was on my way to town. I heard hurried footsteps behind me and then her voice calling me by name. She caught up with me, and without any preliminary she said, "I know that you are Jewish. You should not be afraid of me. I only want to help."

I froze. I could hardly breathe. This meant the end.

Before I could recover, she continued, "You see, you really can trust me. I am Jewish too, and Lusia is not my niece, but my daughter." She went on to say that often through the wall she heard Marta abusing me, that she felt sorry for me, that all she wanted was to comfort me.

"The man who used to visit you," she said, "was your father. You look so much alike that you can't deny it."

She was right. Why had none of us ever considered this resemblance as a possible giveaway? Her statement instantly convinced me that it could have been. She sounded sincere. But how could I possibly trust her? Did she want to trap me? I stared at her and saw for the first time that despite her bleached blond hair she did look Jewish. It was possible, quite possible, that she really did want to help me. After all, she had exposed herself, too. There was something appealing in her approach and her whole manner and I was in such need of comfort that I had an impulse to throw my arms around her and cry. Yet some inner power prevented me from doing so. I remembered my father's last injunction never to admit that I was Jewish, and instead of confessing I heard myself say, "I don't know what you are talking about. I don't understand you at all." I tried to speak calmly, and I was relieved to hear her reply, "I know that you can keep a secret. That is why I told you about us. You don't have to admit a thing, but we can still be friends." "Oh, yes, of course we can be friends," I said, excused myself, and moved quickly away.

My rebuff did not discourage her. On the contrary, she began visiting me in our part of the house. Each time she came she would bring me something—a piece of candy, an apple, a roll. She paid her visits only when Marta was out, but she never again brought up the subject of my Jewishness.

This strange relationship did not go on unnoticed. One day, in front of his mother, Jurek asked innocently, "Why are you such good friends with that old woman?" Marta, predictably enough, was upset, and demanded to know why I had never mentioned the visits to her. I refused to explain. Once again I was afraid that if she knew someone suspected me of being Jewish, she would throw me out.

For the time being Marta dropped the subject. When the children were not about she began scolding me again. "Don't you know how dangerous it is to be friendly with strangers? Don't you know that woman's niece has close ties with the Germans? Both of them may be Nazi collaborators."

While I knew that Marta was right, I could not tell her what I knew, nor did I think it would be safe to tell our neighbor what Marta had said. I felt most miserable and promised to avoid the woman.

From then on, I told Marta whenever the neighbor came. She felt as strongly as I did that although we should discourage her advances, we should not antagonize her. Eventually her visits became less frequent, even though she never gave them up entirely. I had the feeling that her approach to me was sincere, and the more I thought about it the more amazed I was that she had trusted me with her secret. That had been reckless of her, even though I had no intention of betraying her. The whole incident caught me in the middle, and burdened me with one more thing that I must not mention to anybody.

Oddly enough, at about the same time someone else shared a secret with me. This was Stanislaw, who by degrees had become a special friend of mine. He was a tall, imposing man, with a powerful and authoritative voice. He treated me with much consideration, which made me feel grown-up, almost a grand lady. He never tired of telling me stories about his life, and he told them over and over again, embellishing and altering them in the retelling. I enjoyed the way they changed, even the way a new version of a story might wholly contradict an earlier one. The drama of his tales and his gift for conjuring up beautiful and vivid images were what mattered.

Stanislaw often told me how much he liked my company, and sometimes he wondered about my Jewishness: "Look at yourself! You cannot be Jewish!" he would exclaim. And yet whenever he spoke to me about his anti-Jewish sentiments he did so in such an apologetic way that I could not feel upset or resentful. It was in the course of one of these curious conversations that he began speaking about his son-in-law Tosiek, of whom he disapproved. It wasn't just that Tosiek was socially unworthy of Marta, it was because his mother had been born Jewish. She had been orphaned as a little girl and the nuns who adopted her brought her up as a Catholic. At sixteen they married her to Tosiek's father. Although she had been a devout Catholic for almost sixty years, to Stanislaw she was nothing but a "plain Jewess." I was flattered that Stanislaw had confided this secret to me. I knew that if it should become public, both Tosiek and his mother would be in grave danger. At the same time, his resentment toward Jews hurt me because it extended to Tosiek, of whom I was so fond. Perhaps it would eventually extend to me, too.

Still, he went on treating me with the greatest kindness and courtesy. Sometimes, because of the special relationship that Marta had with her father, I was tempted to tell him how badly she treated me. She who perpetually criticized the failings of others was tolerant of Stanislaw's idiosyncracies. She never showed him disrespect, never contradicted him. And when he said to her, as I knew he did, "Send me Krysia, she makes me forget my pain," she would comply. Sometimes, if two or three days had elapsed since my last visit, she would even order me to go and see him. I was of course delighted, but I tried to conceal my delight because I was afraid that if she knew how much I enjoyed these visits she might put a stop to them.

Visits to Stanislaw gave me a chance to see the Rubins too, and also to shop, visit the library, and go to church. I had come to look forward eagerly to being in a church, not only because there I could eat in private, but also because the quiet and peace were soothing. Inside a church I felt like neither a Christian nor a Jew, but only a human being, who had a terrible need to confide in someone. In the stillness I could whisper my secrets without fear, and whether it was a Christian or a Jewish God who listened to me did not matter. What mattered was that I had someone to confide in, and that he was listening.

Marta developed a cough that refused to go away. Even though her doctor reassured her that she was not seriously ill she was worried and her spirits underwent a marked decline. Her energy deserted her. She began to tire more easily and rest more often, and of course her poor health did not improve her disposition. One day she came home looking as if she could not wait to unleash the fury that possessed her—and indeed she began shouting at me as soon as she had come through the door. According to Marta, someone had asked her, "Are you starving your niece to death, so the poor thing has to buy bread?" Shaking her fist in my face, Martha shrieked, "What is the matter with you? Are you trying to shame me? Do you want to ruin my reputation?"

I would have admitted my guilt if she had given me a chance, but she kept on screaming until she started coughing. Even that did not stop her, and she continued in a gasping voice. "Look what you are doing to me! Why are you doing it? Why?" Shaken, I kept quiet, thinking that she might actually die and that I would be blamed. I did not feel sorry for her, just afraid, even after she had to go to her bed and lie down. Without much thought I took her a glass of water, which she vigorously pushed away. For some time she went on alternately shrieking and gasping for breath. Very slowly she managed to calm down. For the rest of the day I felt depleted, tired of struggling, tired of living. I was sunk deep in depression, and told myself that I simply did not care any more about anything, about my parents or my sister or myself, or whether any of us lived or died.

When Tosiek came home he noticed that something had happened. Marta was too weak to talk, and as usual I preferred to remain silent. So the children told him. Because of Marta's condition, Tosiek said nothing, but his manner toward me was particularly friendly. This was his way of offering me comfort.

For a while after that I avoided all stores. Eventually I did go out again to buy bread, but I became much more cautious, taking care to make all my purchases as far away from our section of town as possible. An extra layer of secretiveness, combined with a fear of discovery, became part of my being. All my life revolved around hiding; hiding thoughts, hiding feelings, hiding my activities, hiding information. Sometimes I felt like a sort of fearful automaton, always on the alert, always dreading that something fatal might be revealed.

No matter how I spent my days, I spent the evenings listening for train whistles. Their sounds gave a positive dimension to my life. One of them announced the nightly arrival of Tosiek. Other whistles brought a promise, signaling the possibility that someone would come to take me away. The last train arrived at ten o'clock. Half an hour later I knew that that night was not to be the night, and I would have to wait for tomorrow. Why I was convinced that I would be rescued at night I do not know. The sound of train whistles coming through the dark stirred in me stronger expectations and more vivid dreams than those I heard during the day.

Then one evening, unexpectedly, Wojtek arrived. He was on his way to a new work assignment, and he came to visit with Maria and Stanislaw before going on. Marta asked him to stay for dinner. I knew that he must have a message for me but dared not look at him, and he pretended to be barely aware of my presence. By the end of the meal my head was swimming, and I could not follow what was being said. At last, more eagerly than usual, I took the dishes to the kitchen. Alone, I could at least smile as I tried to think of some way to communicate with Wojtek. Then I heard him say that he was going to the kitchen for water. As soon as he had joined me there, he murmured quickly, "All is well, your sister will come for you soon. Don't tell anyone. Don't worry." That was all he said. I had no time to answer. He returned to the other room with a glass of water.

It took me a while to think. I washed the dishes, unaware of what I was doing. By the time I finished and returned to the other room, Wojtek was gone. I would have loved to talk to him, but I dared not ask Marta for permission to visit her parents. I kept silent. I felt elated even though I had no idea how soon I would be leaving, and I was afraid to say a word that could have betrayed my state of mind.

For a few days after Wojtek's visit I avoided even the Rubins, because I simply did not trust myself with the secret. They would have seen Wojtek, even perhaps talked to him, and if they noticed a change in me they might associate it with something he had said. I did not visit them until I was feeling calmer, and when Stefan questioned me about Wojtek I gave the official version, that he had simply stopped by on his way to another job. Stefan did not probe further. In a sense he needed me more than I needed him and he wasn't going to do anything that might antagonize me.

After my brief elation, life moved back into its usual routine. Outwardly there were no changes, only now there was some support for my hopes and dreams. There was soon going to be an end to my anxious isolation, and this made it easier to bear.

A totally uneventful day preceded my last evening in Otwock. We had just finished eating, and it was probably eight-thirty or so. Marta was resting on the bed. She looked drawn and yellow, and her cough had changed from bad to worse. Tosiek was at home,

I felt relaxed. That evening as always, I listened to the whistles and, as always, I kept thinking, "Maybe tonight?"

Then there was a knock, and a moment later my sister came into the room. She looked so grown-up, so pretty, as she stood there smiling, that for a moment I was paralyzed with happiness. I had imagined this scene so often that perhaps I was imagining it still. But she was wearing clothes I had never seen before and could not have imagined. And then I felt her arms around me, and heard her explaining to the others that she had come to take me with her. My mother was sick again and wanted to see me, so I was going to visit her for a week and then I would come back. She gave me another hug, and told me to pack only some of my clothes and leave the rest. Because I would be gone for only a week, there was no point in taking all of them. I moved in a trance, doing what she told me, packing less than half of the few clothes I owned. This was what I had been waiting for and dreaming about, and now it was really happening. It was happening so suddenly that I felt overwhelmed.

Much later, my sister explained that leaving some of my clothes was a precautionary measure to make sure that Marta and Tosiek would not suspect that I was leaving them permanently. In Otwock we were at their mercy. There was no way of guessing what actions they might take if they knew they were being deprived of an income they had come to depend on.

My sister's manner that evening was very friendly. She inquired about Marta's health, and gave some candy to the children. Politely she declined an invitation to stay overnight. We had to catch the next train, she said. After that everything happened very fast. I said good-bye. I do not remember how. I only remember being in a terrible hurry, as if I could not bear to remain there one minute longer.

Outside in the cold air, I regained some of my

senses. "I have to say good-bye to the Rubins and Stanislaw," I said.

"Impossible," my sister firmly told me. "We go straight to the station." I burst out crying, but I was not sure why. "Cry quietly," she ordered. I followed her blindly, still crying. But it was a resigned weeping full of happiness and relief. I cried like that all the way to the station, where Wojtek was waiting for us. As we boarded the train, I did not even look back.

CHAPTER FIVE

———◆◆———

Reunion

DURING the journey I was dizzy with excitement. All my troubles vanished. The possibility of being taken off the train never entered my mind, and I hardly noticed that this was a long, uncomfortable trip, with many unscheduled stops. We rode through the night sitting on hard benches, and we were among the fortunate ones. Those who boarded the train after us had to find places on the floor.

As the night wore on, many of the passengers slept, and some of them snored loudly. The cars were filled to capacity, and all the windows were shut tight against the cold. The sheer number of people, densely packed, gave rise to a strong odor that in normal circumstances would have been unbearable to me. But that night my excitement shielded me from all negative impressions. Even the dry bread the three of us shared tasted delicious, as did the weak and watery tea that Wojtek bought for us. I kept looking at my sister and squeezing her hand, not yet convinced that this was really happening. We did not talk, knowing that an unguarded remark might arouse suspicion. I welcomed this enforced silence. I preferred to luxuriate in happy fantasies, vivid enough to keep me from falling asleep.

It was morning when we reached Kielce. We stepped off the train and set out on what proved to be a long walk. All I wanted to do was listen, and I urged my sister to talk about anything and everything. With a happy smile, she assumed the role of guide to Kielce. The railroad station was the center of the city, and also the starting point for the main avenue, Kolejowa, both sides of which were lined with new structures. Some of these were office buildings, some were luxury apartments. On the ground floor most of them had beautiful shops. A number of attractive side streets branched off Kolejowa, and they too were lined with expensive shops and elegant living quarters. Kielce, though smaller than Lublin, was a big city by local standards.

Soon I would discover that except for the compact, modern section immediately surrounding the station, the city was a disorderly jumble of the rural and the urban. The roads were narrow and winding, paved with cobblestones or not paved at all, and nearly all the wooden or stone houses were no more than one story high. Most had no running water, and none had indoor toilets. Here and there, scattered among the houses, were vegetable gardens, cultivated fields, and open meadows. It was in this humble, muddled part of Kielce that my family had found refuge.

On that first morning the physical surroundings made hardly any impression on me. I was interested only in hearing about my family. My sister explained that she worked as a cashier in a combination club and canteen for German officers—a most desirable job, because it gave her protection against the threat of deportation to Germany. She had been working there less than two months, not long enough to be entitled even to a short vacation. About a week before she had sprained her ankle, and got a letter from a doctor recommending that she be allowed a leave of absence.

"If I had not sprained my ankle, you would have had to stay much longer in Otwock," she told me. Concerned only with my own good fortune, I paid no attention to my sister's discomfort. Again and again she had to remind me to walk more slowly.

Finally, after what seemed a very long time, we reached the Homars' place, and my parents' out-stretched arms. I was squeezed and hugged, and moved from my father to my mother and back to my father and then to my mother again. I did not mind. I was ecstatic. I felt completely fulfilled, thoroughly happy. Everything looked so promising and so free of suffering that all thoughts of danger disappeared and nothing mattered but the reunion. My mother cried and cried. My father smiled and kept looking at me intensely, as if he wanted to know how I really *was*, how I felt inside.

"Oh, my Krysia, how little and skinny you are!" my mother kept repeating. Soon she placed food in front of me and tried to make me eat. But I, who was forever hungry, could not swallow. Nor could I speak.

Of course I was introduced to all the members of the Homar family, but at first I did not pay much attention to them. I was interested only in my par-ents, and all I could do was hug them and smile.

After the first excitement came exhaustion. All my strength left me, and for more than a week after the reunion I slept long hours and felt perpetually tired. It was as if I was recuperating from a prolonged illness. My parents hovered over me, and my moth-er, in particular, kept hugging me, kept laughing and crying. It was good to feel like a child again, to *be* a child, loved, protected, and not to have to talk about anything serious or upsetting. I was particu-larly grateful that no one asked me about my life in Otwock. The memory of the humiliation and despair I had suffered there stayed with me for years. I could not talk about Otwock then, or at any other time. The scars were too deep.

By slow degrees, though, I did regain my usual way of feeling and behaving. I became aware of the new surrounding, the new arrangements, and the new people—became interested in understanding and knowing as much as possible about the place and about the life that I was to share.

Our apartment was part of a compound of one-story structures, some built of wood, some of stone, huddled together around an open space and a partly enclosed courtyard in which children, chickens, and goats ran freely. Behind these houses were meadows with a stream running through. All the buildings and the meadows were owned by a rigid, stingy old man, who lived in one of the houses with the young woman he had recently married. Because the rent was low, and because our landlord hated to part with money, repairs and general maintenance were kept to a minimum. Our compound had no wall other than the walls of the buildings themselves, and where the buildings ended there was a large iron gate. Except for electricity this section of Kielce had no modern facilities. Instead of running water in the house, there was an old-fashioned well, into which we lowered buckets hung on a hook at the end of a long, heavy chain that unwrapped from around a wooden wheel as we turned an iron handle. It was a deep well, lined with concrete, and we children were fascinated by the strange echoes it gave out when we shouted into it.

Fetching water was an accepted daily chore. No running water meant no excessive washing. Because the water was cold, some of us did away with washing altogether. We had warm water for a bath twice a month at the most. No running water also meant no toilets. This meant trips to an outhouse, located as far away from the main living quarters as possible.

Our household included twelve people, all of whom had to fit into two rooms. The larger of the two served as a combination kitchen, dining room, living room, and bedroom; the other was used only as a bedroom. Although both rooms had an entrance, we used only the one leading into the big room. In a corner of this room was a large stove on which all our food was cooked, and which kept the entire place warm. A large table, with wooden chairs and benches, occupied the middle of the room, and five beds, all equipped with feather pillows and comforters, hugged the walls. Squeezed into the same room was a chest of drawers and an old-fashioned wardrobe. To the side underneath the floor, was a cellar, actually no more than an underground hole, three to four feet square, covered by a loose piece of flooring with an iron handle attached to it. Here we kept potatoes and other vegetables which we bought from peasants who sold them by the sack.

The second room was smaller than the first, furnished with two beds, a crib, a table and chairs, a second chest of drawers, and a second wardrobe. Curtains and floor coverings were an unheard-of luxury. Floors were made of bare wood, and to keep them clean they were scrubbed on hands and knees. Personal washing and laundry were all done in the big room, which was the center for all our other activities as well. There was a small iron stove in the second room, but it was lighted only in unusually cold weather. Wood and coal were expensive, and any heat in addition to that provided by the kitchen stove was considered a luxury.

In Kielce, my parents did not officially exist. After their arrival they had decided that it would simplify matters if their presence was kept secret. My sister, as I would be later, had been introduced as an orphan and a relative of the family. She and I passed as Poles and were free to come and go, while my parents never left the house even at night.

Behind the second and unused entrance to our apartment was a small alcove, built out of loose wood planks, where we kept a pail that my parents used as a toilet. Before I joined them it was my sister's job to empty the pail at night. When I came I was eager to help, and quite naturally offered to take over the duty of emptying the pail. I was glad to do it. Neither my sister nor I ever looked upon this task as demeaning; we saw it as just another chore.

In my eagerness to be useful I kept following my mother, who took pleasure in letting me do things with her. She also devoted a great deal of time and energy to putting me back into shape. She cried and complained as she examined my head full of lice, but instead of despairing she waged a vigorous battle against the infestation. Indeed, my hair was under constant attack. First she poured lighter fluid all over it. That got rid of some of the problem, but even after several repetitions of the treatment success was only partial. Then, embarrassed, I had to go to the local pharmacy for new remedies, some of which made my skull burn, others of which left me with an itch. But my mother was singleminded and determined, and to my complaints she would only reiterate, "Krysia, don't bother me, never mind the pain, all that matters is to be rid of that zoo." She returned to the attack with renewed energy, and fought on until she won the battle at last. After it was over my hair was temporarily darker and had lost some of its curly quality and its luster, but the lice were banished, never to come back. Mindful of the other children, my mother kept a careful watch over their heads too, using some of her remedies as a preventive measure on them.

Having succeeded, she was delighted and felt entitled to do some bragging. For that she needed an audience, and she tended to select the most inappropriate occasions, usually mealtimes. Neither my red face nor my father's discreet cough had any effect. In the end, fortunately, she exhausted every possible variation of the story, and my poor head stopped being a subject for table talk.

My parents' confinement to the house decreased the dangers of discovery, but it was not without emotional cost.

Of the two of them, my mother had an easier time. She was in general less demanding and more adaptable than my father. Besides, she could more easily find work within the house, and thus fill most of her time. In addition to taking care of the children, she occupied herself with many simple everyday chores. She not only had the ability to focus wholly on whatever she was doing, she also tended to exaggerate the importance of everything she did. When she had to decide on a particular dish to serve she would discuss the many ways of preparing it. This sort of thing eased the burden of her confinement to the apartment, and indirectly was beneficial for my father as well. My mother insisted that he become a part of her "important" decisions and to please her he listened patiently, here and there making a suggestion, occasionally pointing out some possible alternative. Because of her constant prodding he became involved in many of the household activities. She was not a lazy person and could have managed everything with ease, but there were no other activities open to my father. His becoming involved helped him bear his enforced confinement to the two rooms.

I too tried to make life easier for him, and was happy to agree to any of his requests. Among these were trips to the library, where for a modest fee I borrowed books, mostly Russian or Polish classics. Gently, without any insistence, my father suggested that I share in his reading. I was flattered because he never felt that a book was too difficult for me. Not yet twelve, I began to read Tolstoy, Dostoyevsky, Sienkiewicz, and others. How much I understood is hard to tell. I read these works mostly for the story, but I remember enjoying them very much.

Here, just as in Otwock, my parents felt that it would be safer for me not to attend public school. Constant exposure to Polish children and my relative ignorance about religious matters might be dangerous. Polish children were entitled to a free elementary school education, but school attendance was not compulsory. Besides, in our part of Kielce nonattendance was the rule rather than the exception; for many of the neighborhood children formal education stopped around the age of eleven or twelve. I did not miss school and I had many other duties, which gave me a feeling of accomplishment.

Because my father could not leave the house he could not get a professional haircut, and he let me cut his hair. This was a highly enjoyable activity over which we both joked a lot, he trying to instruct me in the art of haircutting, I at first missing a few edges. Eventually he would not let anyone else touch his hair, and I became the official barber.

My father was as meticulous as ever about his appearance. He dressed with care, shaved every day, and had me take care of his hair at least once a week. He insisted that all of us be just as meticulous. My parents' clothes were old and worn, but always clean and pressed. None of us had more than one pair of shoes, which had to be repaired many times over before we bought a new pair. Not only were they resoled, but also the uppers were patched and repatched, often with one patch on top of another. Winter coats, too, were patched in all the places that began to look threadbare, and so were the rest of our clothes. Those of us who had one complete change of clothes considered themselves well equipped.

For some time I was convinced that Wojtek's mother, Stefa, had two identical dresses, one for every day and one for Sunday. Then I discovered that she owned only a single dress. Each Saturday night, before going to bed, she would brush it with cool coffee that was left from breakfast, and then press it with a hot iron. She claimed that this was the best way to keep a dark dress looking good, and after this treatment it did indeed look newer.

All the Homars made me feel welcome. They were so warm and friendly that I was hurt when I discovered that they were anti-Semitic, and totally uninhibited about being so. Unabashed by my presence, they would talk disparagingly about Jews, and even scold me half jokingly: "Don't be a nosy Jew," "Don't be clumsy like a Jew." I said nothing, but my face must have registered some surprise or opposition or both, because they would then add, "You know that you are not a real Jew. You are not *really* Jewish."

Back in Otwock I had of course been aware of Stanislaw's anti-Semitism, but his was less direct, less open. Usually he let an anti-Semitic remark slip through, or he would pay me a compliment for being exactly like a Christian. At other times he would try to justify his attitude toward Jews. The Homars never even tried to deny that they hated the "real" Jew, and insisted that such a Jew was everything bad and evil. At the same time they liked all four of us. I liked them too and was grateful for their protection, but I found their attitude as bewildering as it was upsetting.

My father tried to explain that the Homars, like most Poles, took anti-Semitism for granted. For them it was all relatively simple: they hated Jews because "they were greedy, dishonest, and in general a nuisance to the Christian community." This simple argument did not satisfy me. I couldn't sort out the many contradictions that were a part of our situation. I kept wondering who the "real" Jews were.

My father did his best to enlighten me. "The 'real' Jew," he explained, "is not real at all." He believed that the Homars hated an abstraction, the stereotype of the Jew, but not actual people like us, who happened to be Jewish. Our daily contacts were free of any personal animosity, and indeed bonds of unmistakable affection developed between us and the Homars. Aware of this apparent discrepancy, they emphasized that we were not like other Jews, but special and different, so they had no problems in treating us well.

In a way they were right. We were not "typically Jewish," we did not comform to the image that phrase evoked for them. It did not matter that they had perhaps never encountered anyone who did conform to the image. That was irrelevant. They simply treated us as an exception, which allowed them to keep their anti-Semitism intact.

But this too was only a partial explanation. After all, they had not known us before we joined their household. When they first agreed to take us in, they must have believed they would be risking their lives to protect "real" Jews, whom they despised and detested. I felt as confused as ever, and my father conceded that not everything in life made sense. Of course the Homars knew, just like everyone else, that helping Jews was punishable by death, he told me. But he insisted that we were fortunate precisely because they did not—or did not *want* to—fully grasp the implications of what their protection of us could mean for themselves.

The Homars' needs were modest, but even so the combined salaries of all the working members of the family could not cover their expenses. So they had decided to seize the opportunity presented by the Nazi occupation and keep "cats"—an expression used for Jews who tried to survive by passing. To provide shelter for Jews who in turn would support them seemed a perfect solution to their financial problems. And so they never tried to suggest that our arrangement was anything but a business proposition. By helping us they were shielding themselves from hunger and economic uncertainty. In a sense we were only a means to an important end, a means that could be justified only by this end.

In return for their protection, we had to feed the entire family and pay the rent. It was a large family, extending over four generations. The oldest, Helena, refused to be supported by us or anyone else, and worked to support herself. Next in age was Helena's widowed daughter-in-law, Stefa. Stefa had three children, Wojtek, Tadek, and Basia. Basia, sixteen and the youngest of the three, was a pretty girl, with brown hair, brown eyes, a slightly turned-up nose, and a good figure. She had an even disposition with few desires and few aspirations. As with all members of the family, Basia's formal education had ended with an elementary-school diploma. She had an unskilled job in a glass factory. Each morning she would leave for work, and when she returned in the evening she would eat and go to sleep. She had few friends, and barely ventured beyond the family circle. Her earnings, like those of all the other workers in the family, were very meager. Of her entire family, Basia to me was the least interesting and colorful.

Wojtek, who had arranged our trip to Kielce, was a few years older than Basia. Tadek, the oldest of Stefa's children, was married to Ziutka, who was Marta's sister. The children, Jadwiga and Waldek, belonged to them, and this young family of four shared the little room. The rest of us slept in the larger one.

We lived among people for whom the biggest expense—almost the only expense—was food. Because we paid for the rent as well as the food, the Homars were relieved of almost all financial responsibilities. We had brought with us a substantial amount of gold and jewelry, some of which we exchanged for cash on the black market. No one could survive on the wages paid by the Nazis, so it was not unusual for people to engage in black-market operations or to sell personal possessions to supplement their income. At work, my sister met Poles who were glad to buy gold or jewelry from her.

Our diet was modest. White bread could be purchased only on the black market and was too costly for us. Our breakfast consisted of dark bread, usually without anything on it, and tea or imitation coffee with only a little milk, sweetened with saccharine because it was cheaper than sugar. For lunch, which was the main meal, we had a vegetable soup that generally included dried peas, beans, lentils, or the like. These soups were more often than not meatless, but they were thick and fairly filling, and they were followed by potatoes. Again, because fat of any kind was just as expensive as meat, the potatoes, whether mashed or just plain boiled, were served with very little or no fat at all. The evening meal consisted of leftover soup and dark bread, and if no soup was left we simply ate bread.

We all agreed that the quality of food was not an issue. What was more important was its steady supply and quantity. My father insisted that none of us would go hungry, but we could not indulge in luxuries. No one knew when the war would be over; we had to make sure that our money and other negotiable possessions lasted as long as possible.

None of us suffered from lack of appetite, and the amount of food we consumed was enormous. For breakfast alone we would finish two huge loaves of dark bread, each weighing more than four pounds. Occasionally, as a special treat, we had butter to put on it. Being scarce and a luxury, the butter had to be distributed fairly among all of us. But how do you divide less than one eighth of a pound of butter among so many hungry people? Everyone agreed that my father would be fair and that he had the skill to carry out this responsibility.

It would have been a challenge to anyone's ingenuity. There were more than eight pounds of bread to that less than an eighth of a pound of butter. The problem was to put butter on every slice. To reduce the amount of surface to be covered by the butter, the bread had to be cut thick, but the real test came in the next stage. My father would hold a slice of bread in one hand and a knife with a mere drop of butter on it in the other. Then the bread and the buttered knife would come closer and closer without touching. When finally they met, the knife barely patted the bread. The trick was to leave whatever butter there was on top and not push any of it below the surface. To accomplish this, the movement of the knife had to be swift, gentle, and even. Having invented this method, my father became a true expert, whose skill no one else could equal. He only performed this task twice a week at the most. The rest of the time the bread had nothing on it.

We ate meat only on Sundays. About two pounds had to feed all of us, making it more a symbol than a reality. The small piece that each of us was entitled to only teased our appetite, but this did not diminish its importance. An added complication had to do with who was to cook it. The only two people willing to take on the responsibility were my mother and Stefa. Both were good cooks, but when Stefa took charge the meat dwindled as it cooked because she hardly took into consideration the needs of the rest of us, and kept sampling until there was almost nothing left. We all knew about Stefa's weakness, but were too embarrassed to discuss it. At the same time everybody joined in devising ingenious ways to keep her away from the stove when the time came to start the precious meat cooking. Whenever my mother succeeded in starting, Stefa would not interfere.

Unlike the rest of us, Stefa was reluctant to admit that she had a healthy appetite. She preferred to eat when others were not around. One night, shortly after my arrival, a gentle noise woke me up. I saw

Stefa in her nightgown, her long hair hanging loose, hands stretched in front of her, moving slowly and gracefully in the direction of the stove. Occasionally she would stop and glance around quickly; then she proceeded to her destination. I held my breath, too scared to say anything, but fascinated as well. I had heard many stories about sleepwalkers and believed one should never disturb them, and so I only watched. After Stefa reached the stove, she moved directly to a pot with some leftover soup in it. Throwing one last, quick glance around the room, she proceeded to eat the soup—greedily, but with a minimum of noise. Once finished, she turned around, and as slowly and gracefully as before she made her way back to bed.

My father laughed when I told him about it. Stefa walked in her sleep only when there were leftovers, particularly if they were from one of her favorite dishes.

Stefa and her family had moved to Kielce from Warsaw after the death of her husband in 1939. He'd had a great love for the theater and had spent most of his adult life working as a stage hand for the National Theater. Ironically, a backstage accident led to his death. As a young man he had been active in Poland's liberation movement, a period of his life on which the Homars dwelt fondly. According to them he had been an important underground figure, whom the Germans failed to trap despite repeated desperate efforts. He once had blithely joined the Germans in an exhaustive search for himself. When Poland gained independence after World War I, he was decorated with the Virtuti Militari Cross, the nation's most distinguished award for heroism.

Stefa was now in her midfifties. She was an attractive woman, tall and slim, with regular features and long, graying hair arranged in a knot at the nape of her neck. Her straight posture and the slow, precise way she moved gave her an air of great dignity. She also conveyed the impression of someone content with her lot, someone relaxed, never anxious and never in any particular hurry. In fact, everything she did—working, walking, talking, or thinking—she did slowly.

Another of her outstanding characteristics was a vivid imagination coupled with a lack of concern for the truth. She loved to tell stories, most of which were full of inconsistencies and contradictions. Stefa's lies were not self-serving, nor did they seem to have any other purpose beyond the expression of her fantasies. She was a kind, well-meaning person who tried to be helpful, even though her help was clumsy and inefficient. I never heard her express a single independent opinion.

At first I had felt flattered when Stefa showered me with her stories, but I soon became aware that they were repetitious, dull, and not to be taken seriously. I continued to listen politely, however, and to pretend that I enjoyed and believed them. My parents insisted that I should never annoy or antagonize a Pole, and I scrupulously followed the rule. To have done otherwise would have been dangerous. Besides, as time went on my attitude toward Stefa changed. I became increasingly aware of her positive characteristics, her shortcomings came to seem unimportant, and soon I was genuinely fond of her.

Helena, Stefa's mother-in-law, was at least eighty, and to me, she looked one hundred or more. She was thin, stooped, and bony, with a face like a shriveled apple. The layers upon layers of wrinkles obliterated her features, and only after a while did I notice her lively and intelligent gray eyes and learn that her fragile appearance was deceptive. In fact, she possessed an energetic, spirited personality and an active mind. She was lively, witty, and known for her sharp tongue. She was strongwilled too, and always ready to express an opinion. More often than not, however, she tended to emphasize the positive aspects of life, and even in her criticisms and condemnations there was no real malice. She did, though, detest pretense.

Although she was basically a warm person and clearly felt affection for most of us, including my family, she did not make a show of it. To display affection or kindness would have spoiled the image she was trying to project; it would have represented a weakness, which she equated with sin. She preferred, in short, to hide her emotions, and half seriously and half jokingly she behaved as if she were disgruntled and sour. She was fiercely independent and refused to let herself be supported by the family or us. Instead, she paid her own way. And she too, even at her age, was a worker. She worked as a professional beggar.

Each morning, regardless of the weather, she left the house to start a long walk to the center of town. She always went to a particular street near the main market, placed an old pillow on the sidewalk against the wall, and sat down there, always in the same spot. Around her sat other beggars, each in his or her customary place. A beggar had a definite and an undisputed right to his territory. If for some reason one of them failed to appear, that place would remain vacant for at least two weeks. Only then would someone with a less advantageous position dare to move to it; if the original occupant came back, the place had to be vacated. This meant that Helena could arrive at any time of the day and still be assured of her old location. She didn't miss a day's work except for illness.

One could always find her sitting there impassively, expressionlessly, her hand lying in her lap, ready to receive alms. She did not beg; she did not talk at all, or thank or bless whoever gave her something. She was proud, professional, wholly businesslike. Whenever one of us approached, she pretended not to know us. She did not have any close ties to the other beggars. She often spoke about them and their tactics with disdain, expressing special contempt for those who whined or wept or exaggeratedly thanked their donors. She regarded her job as an honest one, and she performed it with style and dignity. Her income was relatively high. Market days in particular provided her with a considerable amount of cash. But sometimes people would give her used clothes or food. She kept only the good clothes, and gave some to her family. About food she was very choosy. Unless bread was well wrapped she would feed it to the birds, and half rotten fruit or other damaged offerings she would promptly throw away.

Although she was not embarrassed by her occupation, her family was, and tried to keep it a secret from their neighbors. However, they did not mind accepting her gifts. Helena was generous, but even so, she managed to save. Each week she would exchange her pennies for paper money and put it under her mattress. We all knew where her treasure was, but none of us dared to mention it and she preferred not to discuss her finances. And so she continued to lead an independent life, without loss of freedom or dignity, and even though her family objected to her profession they loved and respected Helena, and did not dream of opposing her.

Helena treated me like an adult. She believed in fresh air and exercise, and in her free time on Sundays, she would say, "Krysia, come and walk with me. It will keep you away from doctors." During one of these walks she confided in me that she had been opposed to our coming to Kielce. "I would not harm a Jew," she said, "but I see no point in going out of my way to help one. Besides, it is outright stupid to risk Christian blood for Jewish blood. No amount of money could pay for that." Then, she added, "You and your family are not like Jews. If they wanted to send you away now, I would not let them." I felt as I did when the others talked this way, glad that she liked us, sad that she disliked Jews. I kept quiet.

I developed a genuine affection for Helena, and was delighted when she asked me to call her Grandma. My parents and sister were fond of her; my father in particular admired her intelligence and spirit.

We had less reason to admire the two other adult members of the Homar family, Tadek and Ziutka. Tadek was Helena's grandson and Stefa's son. At twenty-five he was a poor man, an unskilled railroad worker with a boring job that was also insecure; during his frequent layoffs he had no income whatsoever. And yet, even though Tadek resented his job and all that was connected with it, he did not try to find different and better employment. Indeed, instead of searching for another source of income during the periodic layoffs, he did absolutely nothing. To be sure, if it had been possible to improve his lot without any effort he would have welcomed the opportunity. He sometimes spoke about his dreams of financial success, but he never tried to make them come true.

Tadek did have appealing qualities, however. He was physically attractive, of medium height with an athletic build, and with brown hair, intelligent green eyes, and white teeth that flashed in a ready smile. He was in fact a charming man, and women responded to him as readily as he responded to them. He was good-natured and generous and devoted to his family. He thoroughly enjoyed life, and had a fondness for singing, dancing, drinking, and philandering. He was easygoing and easily distracted. Mixed with his zest for life was a certain impatience that expressed itself in impulsive and even violent acts.

When he did act violently it was because of excessive provocation directly traceable to his wife, Ziutka. When the Homars moved to Kielce Ziutka left her entire family behind. The one person she seemed really to miss was Maria, her mother. Only when she wanted to emphasize her nobility did she refer to Stanislaw, usually without emotion, and she was open about her resentment of Martha. Unlike her sister, Ziutka had only a grammar school education, yet she was well-informed and intelligent—with the possible exception of Helena, the most intelligent member of the Homar family. She was also stubborn, determined, shrewd, and unscrupulous. In fact, it was she who had masterminded our coming, though she preferred to give the impression that it was Tadek's idea. It did not bother her that by bringing us to Kielce she had deprived her sister of an income.

Ziutka was a tall young woman of about twenty-five, fair-haired and brown-eyed, with a well-shaped figure, beautiful legs, and a pretty face. And she made every effort to enhance her natural good looks. At a time when makeup was not generally acceptable and was used by few, Ziutka had a whole supply of creams, rouges, pomades, and other cosmetics. She would frequently skip washing, but she never omitted her makeup. Each morning she would move to her little mirror, which stood on top of a dresser, surrounded by an array of jars and pots and tubes. She would then start applying one layer on top of another, giving each part of her face special and careful attention, moving the mirror closer or farther away with each stage in the process to better evaluate the results of her labors. As she did so she smiled at her reflection, showing marked satisfaction with herself.

Whenever I could I would sit nearby, fascinated by the complicated process. Ziutka never objected to my presence; she seemed on the contrary to enjoy my quiet admiration. Halfway through the job she would ask for my opinion. At times I had to point out that from underneath the makeup and powder on her neck a ring of dirt was showing through. My observation would never throw her off. She would only laugh, apply another layer of makeup or powder, and ask me if the dirt was all covered up. It did not often occur to her that dirt might be best removed by soap and water, to which she turned only as a last resort. She religiously followed this morning ritual, which lasted more than an hour and took precedence over all other domestic activities. Ziutka was almost wholly absorbed in her own needs, and for her family she did as little as possible.

Tadek and Ziutka had a stormy marriage, in which violence was mixed with love. Most of the upheavals could be traced to Ziutka's sharp tongue. In a verbal battle she could always win. Tadek, aware of her superiority in that area, resorted to his own superior weapon, the fist. Their life was filled with quarrels, most of which started with insignificant arguments and ended in Tadek's physical abuse of Ziutka.

Anything could start a quarrel. Tadek might say, "How about bringing me a glass of water?" Ziutka would say, "Get it yourself, you lazy bum." To this he would retort, "You slut, all you do is nag and complain. You bring me that glass of water or I'll show you who's boss around here." Ignoring the danger signals in Tadek's red face and raised voice, and forgetting past disputes, Ziutka would say contemptuously, "Oh, sure, go ahead and threaten me, you stupid bully. Not a brain in your head, nothing going for you but a pair of big dirty fists."

This was an invitation for a beating. Tadek would stand over her, raise one of those fists, and shout, "You really want me to give it to you, you slut?" "Go ahead," she would sneer. "For the last time," he would yell, "will you get the water!" The answer was "No." By now he was blind with rage and his blows fell fast and hard and uncontrollably. Ziutka never defended herself. Instead, she kept her hands close to her face and head. Between the blows, she would continue to call him a bum, a bully, a lazy good-for-nothing. It was as if she was inviting him to abuse her more, and that is what he always did. She usually ended up on the floor, badly bruised, unable to speak, making no sound at all. At that point Tadek would stop.

For a few hours after such a scene, they would ignore each other. But then they would hug and kiss and be full of love. What followed was an idyllic stage of marital harmony that lasted for only a few days, to be followed by another outburst. And so it went, 'round and 'round.

I remember being awakened once in the middle of the night by Ziutka's curses. Before I had time to collect my thoughts, she ran into the big room dressed only in a nightgown, went straight for the window, and jumped out into the courtyard. Tadek followed and jumped after her. Screaming, she ran around the courtyard while he tried to catch her. He grabbed her by the hair, which stopped her, and right there in the middle of the courtyard, he proceeded to hit her repeatedly while she continued to scream. Lights appeared in a number of windows, together with some heads, but both heads and lights vanished once the cause of the commotion had been established.

It was an unwritten code never to interfere in a quarrel of this kind. In our poor neighborhood violence was an accepted pattern, and unless the man was a total pushover, his dominance over his wife had to be periodically reestablished by beatings.

We did not discuss these outbursts among ourselves, following my father's injunction that we must never interfere even when the beating was particularly rough. Stefa and the rest of her family also pretended that nothing was happening. Only when Tadek and Ziutka were not around would Stefa comment that the fights were Ziutka's fault, for being too provocative and too stubborn.

These violent outbursts were in sharp contrast to

the harmonious relations of the rest of the family. The only other really discordant note was Helena's dislike of Ziutka. Helena made no secret of the fact that she considered Ziutka manipulative and untrustworthy, and she refused to talk to her. Helena's resentment was one-sided. Ziutka never said a word against Helena and seemed eager to be friends with her. When it came to intelligence and independence of spirit the two women had much in common. And yet, they never spoke to each other. I never found out what Ziutka had done to deserve Helena's rejection.

For guidance and comfort, Ziutka turned to my father. Whenever she was in deep trouble with her husband she would come and talk to him. Although he gave her what advice he could, he managed to remain on good terms with Tadek, too. Because of our total dependence on the Homars it was essential not to antagonize any member of the family. Fortunately my father had lost none of the tact that had led to his friends and business associates nicknaming him "The Diplomat."

As for the small children, taking care of them was my mother's and my favorite pastime. The little girl, Jadwiga, was two. She had golden hair and sparkling blue eyes, and she was lively, undisciplined, and extremely jealous of her baby brother. Her father adored her, and never missed an opportunity to hug and kiss her. Ziutka, on the other hand, was irritated by what she considered Jadwiga's stubbornness and guile, and constantly scolded her. Even though my mother and I did recognize Jadwiga's shortcomings, we found her very appealing.

Waldek, though, was our special favorite. At eight months he was a chubby baby with big brown eyes that took up almost half his face and were a striking contrast to his golden hair. On either side of his heart-shaped mouth was a dimple that became particularly pronounced when he smiled, and he smiled whenever anybody looked at him. There was something irresistible in Waldek's all-inclusive friendliness. His contentment seemed to be inviting all those around him to partake of his inner happiness; when he smiled, all of him smiled.

Waldek was an easy baby in general. Almost from the beginning of his life he had slept through the night, and he would ask for attention only when he was hungry or otherwise uncomfortable. Eager to take care of him, I learned quickly how to hold him, dress him, and feed him. He would invariably respond with his contagious smile and lock his chubby little arms around my neck. His affection was for me like a soothing medication and to dispel a gloomy mood all I had to do was pick him up. His responsiveness made me forget all my troubles.

My mother felt as strongly about him as I did, and went out of her way to find things to do for him. But one member of the family did not respond to Waldek the way we did. Tadek showed little interest in him. He behaved, in fact, as if he were unaware of his son's existence. From all the rest of us, including his mother, Waldek received unvarying love and attention. Although he was Ziutka's favorite, she expressed her affection inconsistently. One day she would hug and kiss him for what seemed hours on end, only to seem to forget him the next day. She did not mind our intrusion into her role as mother, nor did she ever ask if he had been fed or washed or had his other needs attended to; she simply assumed they had been.

Within the Homars' circle, no frequent or extensive social contacts were expected, and whatever contacts did take place were fleeting and limited to our immediate neighbors. They would exchange greetings and gossip while waiting for their turn at the well or if they accidentally ran into each other while marketing, but such exchanges rarely led to more meaningful relationships. Only on rare occasions would one neighbor drop into another's house and even then, as a rule, just to borrow salt or flour or the like.

Even young people like Basia and Wojtek had few real friends. Toward evening, and only when the weather was good, it was customary for young people from about eight to twenty years of age to congregate in the courtyard or in the meadows behind the houses; some would play ball, some would sing, and others would simply sit around and talk. In bad weather, particularly during the winter, both young and old stayed in their own houses.

Churchgoing was a major social event, and people attended services mostly because it was the thing to do. The Homars conformed to this pattern, and my sister and I followed their example. Usually Helena preferred to go to early mass, alone or accompanied by Stefa, and she would return while the rest of us were still getting ready for ten o'clock mass. On rainy days or in cold weather everybody skipped going to church without giving it much thought.

We lived among poor people who led a dreary, uneventful existence, devoting most of their energy to feeding themselves. This was no simple task. Most of them, like the Homars, had inadequate incomes, and needed special skills to stretch their money as far as it could go. They had to be knowledgeable about where and what to buy, and for how much. They supplemented their food supply by raising chickens or rabbits, in some instances even goats. It was usually the children who took care of the animals. At an early age, many of them stopped attending school and made themselves useful at home. In addition they looked for jobs that would add at least a little to the family income. It is not surprising that neither young nor old had much time or desire for social entertainment.

Ziutka and Tadek, however, did keep up a tenuous friendship with a neighboring couple, Mr. and Mrs. Koziarz. On the rare occasions when they paid the Homars a visit, my parents went into the smaller room. Infrequent though they were, such casual calls were nerve-racking. First there was the possibility, no matter how remote, that one of the visitors might want to come into the next room. When this did in fact happen my parents would have to slip into the alcove attached to it and stay motionless until the Koziarzs left. A more constant threat was the chronic cough that my father had for as long as I remember. In our present situation it was a serious liability, and the fact that it afflicted my father sporadically, but uncontrollably and without warning, made us especially tense.

Tadek and Ziutka tried to discourage Mr. and Mrs. Koziarz from coming, but they knew that doing so too emphatically might make them suspicious, so their rare visits had to continue. When they did come, my sister or I, whose existence was official and acknowledged, would retire to the second room so that if my father had one of his seizures, the cough could be attributed to one of us.

As long as only friendly neighbors dropped in we could cope with this problem. But the situation was changing. It was becoming increasingly likely that our visitors would be the Nazis. They were definitely stepping up the number of raids in search of people who lacked proper papers, some of whom they deported for forced labor in Germany, some of whom just vanished. At first these raids had been limited to public places such as movie houses, railroad stations, and coffee shops. With time they spread to private homes suspected of harboring fugitives. No one could be quite sure when and why a particular house would be searched, and the uncertainty gave rise to a special tension. We agreed that in the event of such a raid my parents would hide in the cellar behind the sacks of potatoes, but because most apartments in the area had such cellars, it was too obvious a hiding place. So the plan was at best makeshift, and gave us no sense of security.

As time went on the Nazis instituted a permanent curfew. The streets had to be cleared by eight o'clock, except for those few Poles whose work demanded that they return home late; they were given special permits. Penalties for breaking the curfew were severe, ranging from a beating to imprisonment and even death. Not surprisingly, the streets were usually empty almost an hour before eight o'clock.

During my first spring in Kielce, on the day before Lent, the Homars decided to celebrate by making the traditional pancakes. In our circumstances, this would be a real indulgence. When we began the preparations we discovered that there was no oil in the house. I volunteered to buy it at a nearby store. It was seven in the evening, and dark. The curfew would not start for an hour, so I had plenty of time. Ziutka offered me her thick warm shawl, which I threw over my shoulders as I ran out the door.

I had to go across our courtyard, through the gate, along the street, past a two-story apartment house, and then through another gate into an orchard, at the far end of which was a house with the store. This was a black-market operation, run by an elderly couple who owned the house and the orchard. Though small it was well-supplied, and local people shopped there whenever they needed something in a hurry.

On that particular evening the street was deserted, but as I moved toward the gate and into the orchard, I noticed near the street lamp opposite the gate a man standing in a provocative position. He wore a uniform and perhaps was a German soldier. I did not dare examine him closely, and the dim light would have prevented me from seeing him clearly in any case. I quickened my steps, entered the orchard, and reached the house. I chatted for a few minutes with the elderly couple and then, with the bottle of oil under my arm, bade them good night.

Only when I had gone out through the orchard gate did I remember the man by the streetlight. A little apprehensive, without looking around, I moved swiftly. Suddenly, with no sound or any other warning, I felt two rough hands take hold of my shoulders and turn me around. They belonged to the man in uniform. We were beyond the pale yellow glow cast by the streetlight. I was too scared to look at him directly. My eyes moved only as far as his mouth, and what I saw petrified me. Around his lips there was a ring of white foam. He kept a firm grip on my shoulders, and without uttering a sound pushed me against the fence, then pulled me toward his body, then pushed me against the fence again. He kept repeating this movement, back and forth, back and forth. I offered no resistance and could make no sound. But as he continued his terrifying ritual, he began to make hideous noises whose meaning I did not understand. My shoulders and then my entire body began to ache. My mind went blank, and a deathly numbness came over me. Yet I could not take my eyes off his mouth. It continued to froth, and its shape gradually became more distorted. My head reached only to the middle of his chest, and each time he pulled me against him I had trouble breathing. I began to gasp for air, I began to feel dizzy, and his shoves and tugs were becoming steadily rougher and more urgent.

With a supreme effort I moved sideways, and managed to slip away from him. He loosened his grip on my shoulders, but continued to clutch the shawl. Without conscious effort I threw it off and ran. I ran and ran with all my might, still silent, still without uttering a word.

I have no idea whether or not he tried to chase me. Aware of nothing, dazed, but still holding the bottle of oil, I reached the house in a state of total exhaustion and collapsed. It took a long time before I could control my sobs and explain what had happened. My mother wept. My father was unusually quiet, as if in a state of shock. Everybody was happy to see me alive. Everybody except Ziutka, who was furious that I had lost her shawl.

CHAPTER SIX

———◆———

A Pattern of Life

WHEN warm weather came I discovered how many children there were in the neighborhood. Toward the end of a sunny day they were scattered all over the meadows in back, the courtyard in front, and the street beyond the gate. From our apartment I could hear their shouting, singing, and laughter.

It had been a long time since I had played with other children. As I listened to the happy clamor I realized how much I missed being a part of such games. From my isolation their gatherings looked exciting, their friendships warm and intimate, and I yearned to join them. Even so, I knew that I could never be as carefree as they were. I had to be on guard, always on guard.

After a while, though, I did hesitantly venture out. They welcomed me without any fuss or questions. Thus encouraged I joined them more and more often, until I became a part of their circle. But as I felt more secure, truly accepted, I realized that their friendships were not as close as I had imagined. They never visited each other's homes and their conversations never touched on their personal feelings or on events that had real meaning in their lives. Their friendships were superficial. In a way

141

this disappointed me, but it also suited my special situation. For no matter how much I might have liked any of my new friends, I could never have been completely honest or open with them, could never have become a "true friend" to anyone.

Although my parents did not prevent me from joining the other children, they emphasized again how important it was never to divulge my secrets, and as a precaution we agreed that I should never even refer to my imaginary past. "Liars have a short memory," they told me. So I talked about my past only when the others asked me questions I had to answer somehow and, knowing I was stepping on shaky ground, I kept my answers as brief and off-hand as possible. The slightest slip could have tragic consequences.

My father also warned me not to react to the anti-Semitic remarks I was bound to hear, and not to resent the children who made them. He insisted, as he had before, that ignorance was responsible for their hatred of Jews, and that they deserved pity rather than hatred in return.

I managed not to hate them, but I could not pity them. I was as hurt by their attitude toward Jews as I was by that of their elders. I never heard them say that they were sorry for the Jews, and I discovered that if they were actually faced with Jewish suffering they acted as if it did not exist.

Once, in town, a Polish friend and I saw a small group of Jewish workers from a local factory walking along in the middle of the road, surrounded by German soldiers with machine guns. They wore tattered clothes of an indefinite, tired, colorless gray that, in a strange way, seemed to blend with their bodies. They looked exhausted, depressed, depleted of energy almost of life itself. Moving listlessly, their eyes mostly stayed fixed on the ground; when they glanced up their eyes had a vacant, empty look, which saw nothing and cared about nothing. They were pathetically shrunken into themselves, totally apart from their surroundings. Occasionally, roughly and contemptuously, a soldier would push one of them with his machine gun, but they continued to move automatically. If dead people could walk, I would expect them to walk that way.

Pointing in their direction, my friend said indifferently, "Jews." Afraid to show my pain, I shrugged and said nothing, but that night I cried tears of helplessness as I described the scene to my parents. "It will soon be over," my father consoled me. I could not feel sure that he believed what he said.

Although my friends were not interested in Jews as living and suffering beings, Jews were a part of their everyday speech, constantly referred to as symbols of greediness, dishonesty, and guile. And yet I played with these Polish children, and valued some of them as friends. It was hard for me to understand and accept that those I thought of as kind, considerate, and helpful, were often the most vehement in their remarks about Jews.

In a sense, they were unconsciously telling me that I was their friend only for as long as they thought I was one of them. I could not doubt that their friendship would turn into denunciation if they knew who I really was.

Janka was a friend to whom I felt especially close. Two years older than I, she was a big, plain-looking girl who felt protective toward me and treated me with special kindness. We enjoyed each other's company, and sometimes we would leave the rest of the children to chat and gossip alone.

One evening, as we were resting on the grass away from the others, she began telling me a story that had to do with Jews catching Christian children, murdering them, and using their blood for matzoh. At first I listened impassively, but then a strong urge came over me to correct her distorted view.

Around us was peace. A sunny day was coming to

a calm, unhurried end. The distant sounds of insects and frogs, the gentle breeze, the clean perfumed air, all made me feel relaxed. I was fond of Janka, and sad that she did not know the truth. She was good and kind, and I was convinced that if she really knew the facts she would certainly change her way of thinking and talking about the Jews. As innocently as I could, I asked, "Do you really believe Jews do that? Have you seen it happen?" I could see that she was startled, and there was a long silence. Then she turned to me and said angrily, "How strange, Krysia, that you should ask such a thing. Everybody knows Jews do that, but they're smart, they do it secretly! So how could I have seen such a thing?"

As she scrutinized me in anger and disbelief, my heart sank. What if she suspected me? I was really scared, too scared to say anything, and my heart pounded heavily through another oppressive silence. Then, with a slightly changed tone, Janka said, "You're still a baby, young and dumb, that is what you are!"

I was relieved, but for days I had terrible fantasies about her denouncing me, and I blamed myself for destroying all of us. Too ashamed and frightened to report this episode to my parents, I waited all alone, in constant agony, convinced that each day would be our last. The anticipated disaster did not happen, but I had learned my lesson. I tried harder than ever not to make any comments at all about Jews, and did not disagree with anything derogatory that was said about them.

And eventually I grew oddly accustomed to anti-Semitic remarks. A slow transformation was taking place in me. It was as if in certain circumstances I lost track of who I really was and began to see myself as a Pole. I became a double person, one private and one public. When I was away from my family I became so engrossed in my public self that I did not have to act the part; I actually felt like the person that I was supposed to be.

There were times when I believed myself to be truly Stefa's niece, as Polish as any of her blood relations. It was not that I really forgot who I was, only that I became able to push my true self into the background.

I liked my new name. Feeling and believing myself to be Krysia Bloch made life easier, and I felt less threatened when Jews were mentioned. I could listen to anti-Semitic stories indifferently, and even laugh heartily with everyone else about some Jewish misfortune. I knew that they were abusing my people, but part of me was like them.

I never talked about these changes to anyone. I was not proud of them. I felt guilty and embarrassed. I felt like a traitor. It was as if, as I gave up my old self, I was giving up my family as well. Sometimes this terrified me, because in truth my family was all I had.

These inconsistent and powerful emotions continued to battle within me, and I did nothing to reverse the process. In part I did not know how to reverse it, and in part I did not want to. It was easier not to. Life moved on, I became increasingly absorbed into my surroundings, and as I did I offered less and less resistance to what was happening to me.

The meadows behind our houses, like the rest of the land, belonged to our landlord. Traditionally, each summer he gave the local children a chance to earn money by helping with the hay harvest. True to his reputation as a miser he paid low wages. Yet this was one of the very few chances the children had to make money, and they were all eagerly waiting for the harvest to begin. I was waiting for it, too, determined like them to add a little to the family income. All I said to my parents was that I thought it would be fun. They warned me that I was not used to such demanding physical labor and that it might be too much for me. But I stuck to my decision, and they allowed me to join the others.

At first, the working arrangement itself seemed as exciting as it was new to me. Two adult men, each swinging a large scythe with both hands, walked slowly in a straight line, cutting the tall grass to the left and to the right, to the left and to the right, in a steady, soothing, seemingly effortless rhythm.

The rest of us, feet bare and rakes in hand, followed close behind, spreading the grass out thin. This we did systematically by raking it into four rows, one after the other. When a particular row was finished we moved to the next one, and then back again. Each time we moved we turned the grass, thus speeding the drying process that turned it into hay. This procedure continued for most of the day. When the sun was low, we started piling the grass into large, loose stacks, thereby preserving whatever dryness had already been achieved. Each morning we pulled the stacks apart and spread the partially cured hay on the field again for further drying. The amount of time the whole process required depended on the weather. Even in ideal conditions the job lasted for at least a week. The finished hay was stored in a nearby barn, and the landlord eventually sold some and kept the rest to feed his own cow and horse.

We performed our jobs amid much playfulness, singing, and joking—warm friendliness and a certain give and take were an important aspect of the work and helped us not to slacken our pace. Our high spirits irritated the landlord, who kept urging us to go on faster. Even when he was not around his hostile eyes must have been watching us from afar, because as soon as someone slowed down a little he would appear out of nowhere, screaming and cursing and threatening to fire the laggard.

At twelve I was smaller and thinner than other children my age, who were, besides, old hands at this kind of work. My parents had been right—I did find it strenuous. I had trouble walking barefoot in the field; the stubble was sharp, and my soles soon became sore and began to bleed. I also developed blisters from working with the heavy rake, and for the first few days just being in the sun for so many hours made me feel dizzy and a little sick.

But I refused to give up, even when the combined physical discomforts were augmented by an emotional strain brought on by the abundance of field mice. I disliked and was afraid of mice. Those that I saw here were newborn babies. Wherever the grass was cut we discovered nests filled with these creatures, tiny, pink, and naked, in most cases with their eyes still shut as they scrambled toward each other for comfort and protection. Their parents had abandoned them, and they looked so pathetic and vulnerable that my dislike and fear soon gave way to grief and compassion. We had strict orders to kill all of them with our rakes. When I refused, my friends took over the job, and I suffered agonies as I watched them do what they had been told to do.

When the work ended at last and payday came, the old man took one look at me and mumbled, "You are too little. I shall pay you half." I protested. My friends stood up for me, telling him what a good worker I was, but all in vain. His answer was, "Half or nothing." I accepted because I had no choice, and then at home shed tears of helpless fury as I gave my parents my meager earnings.

At first they consoled me. As I continued to complain, my father said firmly, "Stop talking about it and forget it. We cannot afford to make a fuss."

I did stop talking about it, but kept remembering, determined that sometime in the future I would take revenge on the old miser. Shortly after the harvest, however, he had a stroke and died. I was convinced that my God had listened to me, and felt not even a twinge of guilt.

* * *

When my working experience was behind me, I
became preoccupied with shopping on the black
market. All Poles had ration books officially entitling
them to designated amounts of various foods. But
frequently the foods were unavailable, and to avoid
starvation most Poles supplemented their diet with
black-market purchases. Because my parents had no
ration books we had to buy a larger proportion of
our food on the black market than most Poles. This
created very few problems. Little attention was paid
to the illegality or danger it entailed, because life
under the Nazis was dangerous whether or not one
engaged in illegal activities. So the black market was
thriving.

One of the focal points for its operations was the
open local market in the center of town. It covered a
large rectangular area, the middle of which was paved
with big cobblestones encircled by wide sidewalks.
The sidewalks in turn were surrounded by two-story
buildings, which in cold weather gave some protection from wind and cold to the vendors, who stayed
close to them. The market offered for sale a great
variety of goods, ranging from food, toys, jewelry,
toilet articles, and clothing, to light furniture.

When possible the sellers of black market products
kept them in baskets, so that in the event of a raid
they could run fast without having to sacrifice their
goods. Despite the sometimes fierce competition, all
merchants were united against their common enemy,
the Germans. Whoever noticed signs of danger would
signal the others, but despite all precautions the Germans sometimes managed to surprise the black-
marketeers. When they did, the punishment varied,
ranging from simple confiscation of goods to fines,
imprisonment, and even deportation. One could never
know what the Germans might decide to do. Still,
any punishment was invariably visited upon the sellers, not the buyers.

There were also stores, operating out of private apartments and houses, in which the same illegal goods were sold at even higher prices. Without benefit of advertisements we all knew about their existence, and we patronized them more often than the official stores. The difference between the two was in fact slight, and most of the official stores carried black-market as well as legal products.

To save money many people preferred to buy on the open market, but doing so called for special skills in order to avoid being cheated. One had to look for good products and know them at sight, and one had to know what the going rate was and then bargain for a fair price. The outcome depended on the buyer's and the seller's adroitness at bargaining, including their ability to read each other's unspoken signals correctly.

The Homars' apartment was a twenty-minute walk from the marketplace. Stefa had previously done all the shopping, but she did not know how to bargain. She was too easily intimidated by aggressive sellers, all too prone to go along with their demands. As a rule she bought poor products at high prices. My mother and father were convinced that I could do a better job, but we had to be careful not to offend Stefa. When my parents first sent me with her they explained that I was going along to help carry what she bought.

Stefa was good-natured and she liked me in any case, so she did not mind when I began to take over other parts of the job. I started by helping her select the products, and then slowly moved into negotiating for prices. Eventually we switched roles and Stefa was glad to be relieved of her duties. She enjoyed coming with me and helping me carry back all the things we had bought together.

Unlike Stefa, I thoroughly enjoyed selecting and bargaining. To me, the whole business of shopping at the market was a challenge and an adventure. My parents' praise for my increasing skill encouraged me to do even better. I kept trying harder, and eventually gained the reputation of a champion bargain hunter.

In the summer of 1943 the Nazis were losing ground both at the front and in the occupied territories. The Polish underground was increasing its opposition, blowing up trains and bridges and killing high-ranking Nazis. Unable to track down those who were responsible, the Germans were becoming more ruthless and more arbitrary in their retaliations against the civilian population. Raids and deportations and killings occurred more frequently and less predictably. In the past they had stayed away from the poorer section of town, but now they were beginning to move their operations into our area as well.

The danger for my parents became acute. Neither the alcove in the second room nor the cellar in the kitchen was an adequate hiding place. Serious consideration had to be given to finding a more satisfactory solution to the problem. Another constant worry was our dwindling funds. The jewelry and gold we had left could not support us for more than a year. We had no way of knowing when the war would end, nor did we know how the Homars would react if they found out that in less than a year we might be penniless. As my parents speculated about the various possibilities, they decided that at best the Homars would ask us to leave. We could not, after all, expect them to support us. But we had nowhere else to go, and leaving without funds would mean death. In the meantime it was important to keep our financial worry to ourselves, and hope that the war would end before our money ran out.

Then an unexpected event further complicated our shaky situation. Tadek became interested in establishing a business of his own. One of his co-workers had introduced him to a successful vodka bootlegger who wanted to expand operations and was looking for someone interested in establishing his own business. Such a person would have to invest all the necessary capital and be responsible for the entire operation, which would be conducted in his own apartment. The bootlegger would teach the investor the necessary skills, put him in touch with the sources of supply, and initially direct him to customers. In return for these services he demanded fifty percent of the profits.

Tadek was enthusiastic about the offer. He believed that such a business, while allowing him to keep his undemanding job, gave him a chance to achieve the great success he dreamed about. Unaware of our financial difficulties, he expected my parents to provide the necessary funds, arguing that the business would end our obligation to support him and his immediate family.

But even if money had been no problem, Tadek's lack of self-control, his impulsiveness and impatience, made the prospects for success doubtful. He liked to drink, and he behaved more violently when under the influence of alcohol. If vodka became so readily available to him, wouldn't he succumb to the temptation of drinking more heavily? In addition, the Homars' apartment could not accommodate all of us plus a bootlegging business, which would in itself add to our danger.

I listened to my parents discussing their worries, and wondered if the situation was not hopeless. We were trapped. Tadek was eager and insistent, and a refusal might infuriate him. My parents had no choice. They agreed to back him, with the gentle stipulation that my father would be his adviser and guide. Through Tadek, my father masterminded the negotiations with the bootlegger, who yielded to his tactful prodding, reduced the initial investment, and agreed to take a third rather than a half of the proceeds.

Tadek's bootlegging proved to be a simple operation. Large containers of ninety-proof vodka were
delivered to his house. All he had to do was dilute it
with water, pour the results into clean bottles, seal
and label the bottles, and sell them. He and Ziutka
became friendlier with their neighbors, all of whom
turned into customers. The neighbors not only increased vodka sales but also gave advance warning of
Nazi raids, so they had time to hide any incriminating evidence. As for profits, neither our own fears
nor Tadek's extravagant hopes materialized. The
earnings were adequate, but far from spectacular.

The business was only a partial success because
Tadek ran it inefficiently. Not only did he make no
effort to find new customers, but he soon also fell
behind in filling existing orders. Both he and Ziutka
refused to plan ahead, emphasizing the present moment and disregarding the future, spending whatever money they had.

Occasionally they would even turn to us for additional loans. Fortunately their demands were modest. And my father comforted himself and us by
saying that we should be glad Tadek's dreams had
not come true. "Who knows?" he mused. "If he had
become really successful and financially secure, he
might have decided we were an unnecessary burden
and risk." This line of reasoning did not end my own
private worries about what would happen if our
money really did run out.

When Tadek established his bootlegging business
it was decided that he and his family would take over
the entire apartment. The rest of us moved to another one, ten minutes' walk away. Our new home
was one of a number of wooden single-story units
huddled together in a horseshoe enclosing a courtyard. Our new apartment was toward the rear center
of the horseshoe, away from the entrance to the
courtyard. To reach the kitchen, one had to pass
through a small windowless anteroom made of loosely

arranged planks. Anybody inside could easily look through the chinks without being observed. Against the wall opposite the entrance to the kitchen was a large stove, which took up about one fifth of the room. Right next to the stove was a bench with a bucket of water resting on it. Past the bench, in the middle of the wall, was a door leading to the only other room. To the right of the door stood a cupboard for pots, dishes, and food. Next to the cupboard, leaning against the wall on the right, was old Helena's bed. The kitchen was too small to accommodate another bed. There was just room enough for a table and chairs, which had to be placed next to the kitchen window. It was a strategic window, affording a view of the entire courtyard.

The rest of us shared the second room. In the middle stood a table surrounded by chairs, and to the side, off toward one corner, was a small cast-iron stove. This was considered a luxury item and lighted only in extremely cold weather. Directly across from the door was a window that faced the street, set too high for anyone to look through from the outside. On the left wall were two beds, one for my mother and father, the other for my sister and me. Stefa's and Basia's bed was on the right, close to the window. During his visits Wojtek slept on a mattress on the floor.

We all felt relieved and happy that my parents' move from the old apartment to the new one had passed unobserved, without any complications. But now we had to decide about building a hiding place. In the second room, next to the bed Stefa and Basia shared, there was another of the old-fashioned wardrobes so common in modest Polish dwellings. Between the wardrobe and the end of the wall was an empty space, and we decided to build the new hiding place here, underneath the floor.

The three men, Wojek, Tadek, and my father, set to work right away. They cut an opening in the floor just large enough to let one adult through at a time, and dug a hole that would accommodate a total of three. The soil was placed in old sacks, to be disposed of after dark. When the hiding place was finished, fresh cuts were visible on the floor. Although paint and dirt rubbed into them made them harder to see, it did not eliminate them. To solve the problem we decided to cover the area with something both light and inconspicuous, which could be removed rapidly and with ease so that my parents could slip into the hole quickly. The choice fell on an old valise, which proved to be an exact fit. We convinced ourselves it looked so ordinary and so natural resting there that it was unlikely to draw the attention of any searcher.

Next we had to solve the problem of reaching this hiding place in time. The Germans descended on a neighborhood swiftly and without warning, because the success of their raids depended largely on the degree of surprise. So my parents began to practice getting in and out of their hole, and eventually succeeded in doing it in less than two minutes. But with someone pounding at the door, even one minute would be a long time.

On the way to our apartment, and attached to one of the wooden shacks, was an unoccupied dog house. We felt that from this spot a dog could signal the approach of a stranger, giving my parents more time. When we asked our new landlord for permission to use his dog house, he agreed immediately. He himself illegally raised pigs, which he slaughtered and sold on the black market, and he decided that a dog would give him warning about raids too, and help him hide any incriminating evidence of his own.

This is how we came to acquire a medium-sized mongrel, whom we called Czarus, Polish for "charming." He was an affectionate animal, who made friends with all of us and all of the neighbors. Helena in particular was very fond of him, and they formed a strong and special attachment. She treated him like a human being, showered him with delicacies brought home from her begging, talked to him at length, and pretended to understand the adoring canine noises he made by way of response.

As a rule Czarus was chained to the dog house. The length of the chain allowed anyone to pass him safely. At the approach of a stranger he would bark, which prepared us for the worst but gave us enough time to glance through the window. If any of us or any of the neighbors passed near him he never barked, and even when those he knew were accompanied by a stranger he kept quiet. We were convinced that he barked loudest and most furiously at the approach of a German.

Our new apartment offered us greater security and more peace, but we missed Waldek and Jadwiga. For my mother the move meant a real deprivation, and to cheer her up we tried to bring the children to our place. Waldek had no carriage, and he was not able to walk the whole distance. We had to carry him most of the way. Because he was a chubby little boy the visits were rare.

I was more fortunate because I could see him and Jadwiga often. Indeed, I fell into the habit of visiting them almost every morning after breakfast. To get to the old apartment I had to pass many fields and cross a bridge built high above a stream. The poor and neglected appearance of the houses seemed diminished by the beauty of their surroundings, and in summer this least desirable section of town assumed a softness and a majesty that transformed it.

Looking down from the bridge I had a floating sensation, and a feeling of awe overcame me. I loved the splendor of the fields and stream and surrounding trees, and the soft, inviting sounds made by birds and insects. As I walked in solitude I joined these music makers by whistling or humming quietly, careful not to disturb their gentle harmony, and breathed in the clean, refreshing smell of the crisp morning air. I felt an inner calm. The real world was far away, untouchable, temporarily forgotten.

Away from my parents I also felt more secure in these surroundings, more relaxed. I loved my visits, and as I reached the old neighborhood I was excited about the warm welcome that I knew awaited me. I was always particularly eager to see Waldek, who remained special.

Curious and intelligent, Waldek could easily become absorbed in the examination of the most ordinary objects. When left with an aluminum pot he would turn it around and around, poke at its smallest indentations, beat on it, and laugh at the resulting sounds. He would also respond with amazed laughter to his somewhat distorted image in the pot's shiny surface.

Each time I entered the kitchen I could hear his bare feet run quickly into my direction, and then I would see him and his chubby outstretched arms. Smilingly, he would hug me as he kept repeating, "Isiu, Isiu, Isiu." He could not pronounce Krysia and I loved what he did to my name. Hugging him and holding him in my arms, I jumped around and around the room. As I kissed him I did not care about his perpetually running nose or the dirt on his face left from the night before.

Jadwiga was less demonstrative than her brother, but she too always hugged me, and smiled so happily that I felt sure she appreciated my being there just as much as Waldek did.

No matter when I arrived, the children were always half naked, dirty, and unfed. Ziutka was usually invisible. What was very visible was a chaotic disorder of piled-up dirty dishes, clothes lying all over the place, unmade beds, and an unlighted stove. First I busied myself with the children, washing, dressing and feeding them. Later, while I tried to create some order out of the chaos, the children stayed close to me, laughing, talking, and playing as they followed me about.

While these domestic duties preoccupied me, my sister continued to work in the club for German officers, a place in the best section of town, where they could eat, drink, and socialize. Except for the club manager, all the employees were Poles. My sister was the youngest, and the others treated her in a protective way. She became a particular favorite of the Polish cook, who kept sending her home with leftover food; it was so much better than anything in our regular diet that it constituted a real treat. My sister was attractive and intelligent and performed her duties diligently, and soon she was promoted and put in charge of food inventory. The job gave her easy access to all the club food, and she started bringing home luxury items such as sugar, meat, and eggs.

During the war we admired anyone who found it possible to steal from the Nazis. Depriving the Germans of anything at all was looked upon as an act of patriotism, a move against the oppressor. At the same time it was risky, and I expected my father to warn my sister about being careful.

But my father, usually sensitive to danger and always aware of it, chose in this instance to push caution aside. Instead of warning her about the risks of stealing, he encouraged her. Instead of pointing out the foolishness of such an enterprise he discussed various techniques for stealing food and the advantages of taking one product rather than another. He knew the dangers but did not seem to consider them.

Was it defiance on my father's part? Did it give him a feeling of independence? Whatever it was, we followed his lead blindly and put all caution aside.

When I thought about it later such behavior seemed almost incomprehensible. It was one of those aberrations so common during the war, but so rare with my father.

Although the risks were great, ironically the gains were minimal. In fact my sister's stealing, even to-. gether with her salary, amounted to very little. Most of her earnings had to be spent on clothes. Unlike the rest of us she could not wear patched-up things. She worked in an elegant place and had to look presentable. After she outgrew what she had brought from Lublin, my mother made over her own clothes for her, but soon these too were inadequate. New clothes had to be bought. My sister's wardrobe consisted of one pair of shoes for the summer and one pair for the winter, my mother's old coat, a suit, two blouses, and a dress. This sounds modest enough, but it constituted a major outlay. And to me she looked elegant. I was proud of my sister and bragged about her to all my friends, telling them tales in which she figured as the manager of a most distinguished and exclusive club.

Her actual working day did not end until seven, and when fall came and the days grew shorter she began to dread the half-hour walk home alone in the dark. The curfew was at eight, but by seven the streets were virtually deserted, especially in our part of town, and one never knew who loitered in the dark. I was delighted when she asked me to meet her at the day's end and keep her company on the walk home.

Of course the two of us never considered just how I could protect her. Actually, after the strange attack from which I had miraculously saved myself, I too was afraid of the dark and empty streets. So I would start out for the officers' club early, when the town was still bustling with life. Once I reached the railroad station and the main avenue where her office was located, I would spend an hour or so walking back and forth in this busy, central area. When I grew tired I would go inside the club and wait until my sister was ready to leave.

These long walks home, during which I felt particularly close to my sister, created an added bond between us. To me she epitomized the height of sophistication, and some of her maturity spilled over, making me feel more grown up. At the same time, as we skipped along through the dark, both of us briefly recaptured childhood, a luxury Jewish children could no longer afford. We learned to appreciate each other more and more, and our relationship became particularly intimate and loving. Only when we were in each other's company could we be completely honest and open. Only then did we feel free to complain about our difficult life. We never did so with our parents because we wanted to protect them from pain and worry.

These walks became a time for exchanging confidences, for the sharing of dreams and hopes. It was at such times that my sister would tell me about her boyfriend, the prisoner of war, who was still in Lublin. My parents had stopped objecting to this relationship, stipulating only that she should never give him our address; it was too risky to let anyone know where we were. And my sister never abused their trust. Her friend's letters would arrive poste restante at the Kielce post office, and she waited for them eagerly, worrying each time there was a delay. The arrival of a letter would change her mood drastically. For days afterward she would be happy, reading and rereading it. His letters gave joy to an otherwise dreary existence. She allowed me to read most of them, which created an additional bond between us.

One day his letters stopped coming. We took turns inquiring at the post office, day after day, but we never heard from him again. We knew from what he had written that he was among the small handful of prisoners in Lublin still left alive. With time we understood that he too must have perished. We never found out how.

My sister suffered quietly. For a long time she was depressed. Still, she had a tremendous need to talk, and although I suffered with her and for her, I was flattered by her trust. I listened sympathetically as she talked about the times they had been together, their plans for the future, his gentleness and affection and understanding. But little by little, for her just as much as for me, his image blurred, and the pain of his loss diminished.

Our walks had to be interrupted whenever Wojtek came to stay with us. He insisted that he would give my sister more protection than a little girl like me. "Come with us, I will defend the two of you," he said. But with Wojtek around the fun of being with my sister was gone, and I preferred to stay home until he left again.

Some of the Polish women who worked with my sister had German lovers and urged her to follow their example. Not to offend them, she said that she had a fiancé who for "certain" reasons had to be frequently away. Noting Wojtek's comings and goings, they were convinced that he must be the one. They also assumed that he was working with the underground. Their conjectures suited my sister very well, and she even encouraged them to think that she too was connected with the underground. This aroused their admiration and approval, and they stopped bothering her about making friends with Germans. It was not unusual for women with German lovers to be on the side of the Polish underground, and their approval of it increased as the Nazis lost ground and the conflict with the underground gained momentum.

I myself looked upon such women as traitors, and was amazed that other Poles should treat them with consideration. One of them, named Teresa, lived close to Ziutka and Tadek. She was exceptionally beautiful, cheerful, and obliging with her favors, and was the mistress of a succession of high-ranking officers, a fact she never tried to conceal. Whenever one of the officers disappeared, another one took his place. Teresa lived in luxury, and because she generously shared her wealth, all the neighbors liked her and treated her well.

After we had moved to our new apartment, Teresa and Ziutka became very friendly, which for Ziutka was a stroke of luck. Along with being a good customer for Tadek's vodka, Teresa was well informed about Nazi moves against the local population and about news from the front. When I asked Ziutka how she could be so friendly with a Nazi collaborator, she laughed and then she said in all seriousness, "Teresa is a great patriot. She uses her Nazi connections to help Poles. Besides, why should she starve?" That was the end of our conversation.

One day Ziutka came to our new apartment out of breath and upset. She had just received disturbing news from Teresa. Apparently a large number of Poles from the underground were hiding in Kielce, where they planned to sabotage many installations and execute important Nazi officials. One such official had in fact been shot the night before as he walked home. As a countermeasure, to apprehend those responsible and check further terrorist acts, the Nazis were planning a large-scale search.

Even as Ziutka was warning us we heard violent barking, and almost immediately the courtyard was swarming with Germans. I rushed to the next room with my parents, who slipped into their hiding place without a word. I replaced the old valise next to the wardrobe. Moments later a group of soldiers burst into the apartment shouting, *"Partisaner, Banditen, Partisaner, Banditen!"* As they spread out and began their search, Stefa joined me in the second room. We were too frightened to look at each other, believing that if we did so we would reveal our fear. The soldiers ignored us. They looked inside the cupboard, under the beds, and inside the beds. Then one of them went to the corner where my parents' hiding place was, placed one leg on either side of the valise, and scrutinized the space between the wardrobe and the wall.

Suddenly we heard my father's suppressed cough. The German jumped back, still without having touched the valise. Frowning, he looked around suspiciously, and then he shook his head as if in disbelief. The suspicious frown was replaced by a smile—a faint, amused, indulgent smile. I froze, using all my self-control not to change my expression, not to sigh with relief. I was too shaken to entertain any rational thoughts, and I am sure Stefa must have felt the same way. She and I did not dare to communicate even with our eyes. After the Nazis had left, the two of us entered the kitchen, still in shock, and neither of us mentioned the cough.

The Germans might return. They often did reappear unexpectedly, so it was safer to wait. Only after an hour did we free my parents from their hiding place. And for an hour my father did not cough again even once.

With time, Wojtek became a special friend to my family. We suspected that he was in love with my sister, to whom he was attentive in a particular way. He behaved like a gentleman, without making any demands on her, never departing from his role as her protector. In a real sense we were at his mercy, but he never took advantage of the fact, and the longer we knew him the more convinced we were of his basic decency and integrity. We came to trust him totally, and when my parents needed help they turned to him rather than to any of the others.

It was clear that the end of the war was nowhere in sight. Our immediate financial resources continued to dwindle, but there was still the store of jewelry and gold we had left with the German commissioner who had taken over our chemical factory in Lublin. We believed that if we arranged for proper identification, he would return it to us. We had to act with great caution, not disclosing fully to anyone how shaky our position was. Still, we were convinced that we could safely entrust this important mission to Wojtek, and explained the details to him. Although he understood and was eager to undertake this task for us, we did not tell even him how bad our financial situation was.

As part of the same trip, my parents wanted Wojtek to visit Bolek, the "tie man." This mission, too, he promised to undertake.

When Wojtek returned he brought with him good news and tragic news.

The commissioner had handed over all our possessions to Wojtek, along with a warm letter expressing his delight that we were alive, and asking us to turn to him for help again if we needed to. He had not even questioned Wojtek as to our whereabouts. That aspect of Wojtek's trip had gone perfectly.

The news about Bolek was shattering. When Wojtek had gone to Bolek's apartment, he found it occupied by strangers. The janitor had told him what happened.

In the middle of the night, the SS had stormed into Bolek's apartment and rounded up everybody there. They shot the others on the spot, but took Bolek to prison. When he protested that his friend, a high ranking officer, should be notified, he was told that the man refused to see him. Bolek was put in solitary confinement. For three days no one came to see him and he was given no food. On the fourth day he had a Nazi visitor, who introduced himself as a friend, someone who was concerned about Bolek's fate. He explained that the officer who had been Bolek's protector refused to have anything to do with him—that he had in fact given free rein to those who had arrested Bolek. The visitor went on to explain that before executing Bolek the Germans intended to torture him in order to learn the whereabouts of all the Jews he had been helping.

Thereupon the Nazi visitor took Bolek on a tour

of a variety of torture chambers, explaining what each of the machines and tools could do, and mentioning often that he felt sorry for him. He then returned Bolek to his cell. It was unfortunate, he said, that Bolek would have to suffer so much before his death. The only possible way in which the Nazi felt he himself could be helpful was to give Bolek an opportunity to commit suicide. In the circumstances, he argued, this was the easiest way out. Whereupon he laid a thick rope on Bolek's cot, and left the cell. Within less than an hour, Bolek ended his life.

The poor "tie man" had been caught between two hostile German factions. Those who arrested him had taken advantage of his chief protector's temporary absence. Terrifying him into committing suicide was a diabolically clever tactic; it would spare them from reprisals from the other faction.

Bolek had been so vital, so alive, that it was hard to believe that he had ended his own life. Even in the days when he was poor and struggling he never lost his zest; his love of life had always mingled with strong optimism, a belief that his misfortunes were temporary. It was ironic that success of a sort had come for him at a time when the world was crumbling, and that it had come to an end so tragically.

With Bolek's death one more link to our past was broken.

CHAPTER SEVEN

———◆●◆———

Without Money

WOJTEK'S successful mission to Lublin gave us only a temporary relief from financial worry. Within a few months the old nagging fear returned. Our new funds would not last for long. Ahead lay an indefinite and unpredictable future. Besides having a large house-hold to support, we were recurrently called on to make unexpected "loans" to Tadek's business.

If it had been only a question of feeding the four of us, we could have cut down on our expenses. But we could not ask the Homars, who had taken us in because they did not want to starve, to eat less. My parents were convinced that it would be too risky to let the Homars know about our financial difficulties, and continued to keep them a well-guarded secret. We felt powerless. With my parents confined to the house and my sister already putting in a long work day, what could we do? My sister gave all her earnings to my parents, and she had no time to take on another job. I had the time. The fact that I was twelve did not matter, but because I was small, thin, and much younger looking than my age, no one would give me a real job. I felt inadequate, and blamed my size for our predicament. But my father disagreed. "Even if you could work," he told me, "the pay would be too meager to help us."

Eventually we decided that we would have to conduct some kind of black-market business. My being so small and looking so young could even become an asset in the black market. Children were less likely to be suspected, and if caught they might be less severely punished. Furthermore, I was mature in other ways, and we thought the skills I had acquired in bargaining for black-market products might be another asset. I was delighted. Finally, I thought, I would be of some use.

The idea that I could become active in the black-market venture was only the first step in a series of decisions. We still had to settle on the kind of business and on ways in which it might be conducted. There was hardly a product that was not produced and sold on the black market. We had to find something that would suit our special situation, and then minimize any risk even if it meant less profit.

The attention the Nazis paid to the black market varied and their reactions to it seemed arbitrary, but they were not wholly unpredictable. The risks involved and the punishments differed depending on the particular product. Any transaction involving weapons was punished by death but, in sharp contrast, the selling and buying of used clothes was often ignored entirely. As for food, the illegal sale of meat was a more serious crime than the illegal sale of flour, and making and selling bootleg vodka a more serious crime than selling meat.

My parents were aware of these and other distinctions, and considered all of them before reaching a decision. In the end they settled on the baking and selling of rolls. My mother, who was an excellent baker, would make them at night, and I would sell them the following day. Stefa and I would buy whatever supplies were needed for our business.

Baking and selling rolls, cakes, and breads was a

well-established black-market operation. Anything made out of white flour was an illegal delicacy, and although the ingredients for baked goods were costly as well, there was an abundant supply of them. All the illegal bakers worked at home; some sold their products directly in the open market, others supplied both official and unofficial stores.

We knew that we would be up against stiff competition, and had no illusions about making a high profit. To avert disappointment my father said: "Small profits are better than no profits. We have to be satisfied with little."

No baking business could have been conducted without Stefa's consent, so to make the project attractive to her my parents had offered to share the profits with her half and half. She would be free to do whatever she wanted with her share, and ours would be used to support the household. Not surprisingly, the proposition delighted Stefa, who insisted that as a partner she wanted to play an active role in the business.

The black market was so much a part of everyone's life that there was no need to keep our project a secret from the landlord or neighbors, and Stefa told them that it was she who had decided to start a small baking business. Before we actually set to work, she and I went to the market to investigate the situation, under detailed instructions from my father. First we stood around the salespeople, studying their selling methods. Then we had to decide which kinds of rolls were most popular, and we bought a few of them, took them home, and examined them carefully in terms of weight, shape, and taste. We also made inquiries about the purchase of flour and yeast, and the food coloring we intended to use instead of eggs.

Suppliers of raw materials were easy to find. In our neighborhood alone there were many black-market stores that specialized in such products. Having learned from our previous experience that we made a good team, Stefa and I went from store to store and from one vendor to another, comparing prices. She stayed in the background while I did the bargaining and the actual buying.

My parents felt that I should do the selling, but because Stefa was so eager to be helpful we had to be careful not to offend her. And so my father tactfully explained that selling was best done by a younger person, adding that the final decision would of course be Stefa's. In fact she was relieved not to have to do the selling, and thanked my father for being so considerate.

We agreed that it would be best to start out on a modest scale, and that the best time for launching the venture would be a Thursday, the busiest market day. The November Thursday we had chosen proved to be unusually cold. As I, not yet a teen-ager, was leaving with my basket of freshly baked rolls to start my career as an illegal salesperson, my mother hugged me tightly, unable to suppress a sigh. My father's parting words were: "Never fight with anyone, no matter what. Do not offend anyone. Be very careful!" I set out in a state of high excitement, but my notion that I was embarking on an adventure was soon replaced by doubts and fear. I wondered how I would do it. What if the other sellers chased me away? What if I could not sell a single roll?

As I walked on, I understood for the first time that selling on the black market would be entirely different from buying on the black market. To obtain the highest price possible would surely be more difficult than bargaining as a buyer, who could always turn away and look for a lower price. Only then did it occur to me that none of my buying experiences had really prepared me for the role of seller. I had a numb feeling that I would not be able to play it.

I wanted very badly to turn back and forget the

whole thing. Then I thought about my parents, how they trusted me and counted on me, and I knew that I could not let them down. I knew that no matter how frightened and miserable I felt, I would still do what I had to do.

My inner struggle had so thoroughly absorbed me that I reached the market sooner than I expected, sooner than I wanted to. Hesitantly, I took a place among the other sellers of baked goods. Most of them seemed indifferent to my presence, as if I was not worth bothering with. A few glanced casually at my basket, but not at me. Then one of them asked sneeringly, "Who bakes those crazy-looking things?" "My aunt," I whispered, and for a moment, as on earlier occasions, I actually believed I was Stefa's niece.

This sort of thing had been happening to me more and more frequently. In some ways I was glad when it happened because it meant that I did not seem to be lying or playing a part. At the same time it scared me and made me feel guilty because it separated me from my real self and from my family.

Then, as I stood there in the cold, imagining myself literally as Stefa's niece, a big fat woman came to my rescue. "Leave the child alone," she snapped. Her imperious, threatening voice was in sharp contrast to her kind and open face. It was the face of someone I could trust and even like. I was grateful and relieved. I said nothing. I had to be careful. I had to stay out of quarrels.

The market was subdivided informally but rigidly into special sections, in each of which only a certain kind of goods was sold. The sellers of baked goods gathered in one such special area, where, with baskets in hand, they kept a sharp lookout for customers. Whenever a potential customer appeared they would run to make a sale. No one interfered with the seller who reached the customer first. The customer, however, could and often did move to another seller.

I was little, thin, and frightened, and instead of running up to an approaching customer, as the others did, I waited for a customer to come to me. Instead of praising my products, as the others did, I kept silent. I suffered and my business suffered with me. Here and there I sold a few rolls, but not nearly so many as those around me did.

Besides that, my warm clothes and my walking about didn't keep me from feeling chilled to the bone. The big woman who had defended me looked my way several times with a kindly smile, and eventually began to urge me on. "Go right up to the customer, get the next sale," she told me, and now some of the others occasionally gave me an encouraging look. Even that small show of kindness made me feel better, though it didn't help me to sell more rolls.

In the afternoon, a few of my co-workers set out for home with empty baskets. The big woman still had some rolls left. She introduced herself as Magda, and went on to give me further bits of helpful information. She pointed out a nearby courtyard where there was an outhouse we could use, and told me about a few shops whose proprietors didn't mind when people stepped inside just to warm up. I felt half frozen already, but Magda said that it wasn't really cold at all. I said little, but I looked at her as gratefully as if she had been an angel sent directly from heaven. Too soon, she left, but as she walked off, she said to the few sellers who remained, "Be nice to the child."

I still had more than half of my rolls, and I was convinced that what I had sold would not nearly cover our expenses. So I stayed on, strengthening myself with a few partly burned rolls that my mother had put in the bottom of the basket for me to eat. The day was slowly approaching its end, and in the dusk the crowds were thinning out. Then a few of the vendors began leaving, with some of their goods unsold. None of them had as much left as I did. I tried to cheer myself up by telling myself that with most of my competitors gone, I would have a better chance to attract buyers. And as if from nowhere a peasant woman appeared, looked at me, smiled, and bought six rolls. Then an old farmer started to argue about price. For a while I stood my ground, but finally I told him, "If you buy a dozen, I'll sell cheap." He agreed. Cold, stubborn, and hungry, I stayed on and made a few additional minor sales. Full dark came, and the market was almost deserted. I decided it was time for me, too, to set out for home.

I was disappointed. My day had not been a success. I was upset because I'd had to sell some rolls cheaply, and even more upset by the eight rolls still left in my basket. I felt like a total failure and blamed myself for not having had enough courage to push and fight. How would I explain what had happened?

In my disappointment, I felt lonely and inadequate. I kept thinking about everyone back in our warm kitchen, which seemed so inviting. And yet I was almost reluctant to return. How would they react to my failure? Would they be as disappointed as I was?

When I entered the kitchen everyone greeted me warmly and was very solicitous. My parents looked relieved and happy to see me, Basia and Helena smiled with approval and made me take off my shoes. While my mother rubbed my half-frozen feet, Stefa poured me a bowl of hot soup. They all crowded around me, asking questions. By way of answer, I emptied the money I had made onto the table. My father began to count, half jokingly and half seriously. When he finished he called out triumphantly, "We have profits, we have profits!" Everybody was excited and nobody paid attention to my unsold rolls. When I pointed to them, all my father said was: "What do you expect? You sold a lot anyway!"

This warm welcome changed my mood. I felt secure and relaxed as I told them about Magda's kindness and about the different customers, imitating the funny ones and the way they haggled. When I came to the bargain rate I'd given the old farmer, my father nodded approvingly. "Smart move," he said. "Better some money than none."

My doubts and fears vanished. Everyone was pleased with what I had done and satisfied by our profits. Even Helena, who was not directly affected by the business, entered into the spirit of the occasion and joined us when we celebrated by eating the leftover rolls.

Whatever profit we made there gratified us, no matter how modest it was. We were convinced that eventually my mother's talents would triumph and bring us a real success. In the meantime, the average number of rolls I sold each day served as a guide to the number my mother baked, though she always doubled the regular amount on the nights before the busiest market days. We continued to proceed cautiously, trying hard not to be left with unsold rolls.

With time I became more comfortable and less frightened about the whole business of selling. Even so I went on being acutely aware of my difference from the other sellers, and knew they must be aware of it too. During those early stages of my selling career I never tried to outrun anyone else, never pushed myself first in front of a customer. Instead I stood back, waiting patiently for my turn. Sometimes customers would notice me and come up to me on their own, and sometimes they paid for my rolls without the customary haggling. I could not help thinking that they felt sorry for me because I was so young and small and shy.

At the beginning, too, the rolls my mother made looked as unprofessional as I must have. Even if I had been more aggressive they could hardly have competed with the products most of the others were selling. By degrees almost all the sellers stopped regarding me with suspicion, suspicion gave way to pity, and then the older women began to be not just friendly but actually motherly. They tried to instruct me in the secrets of their trade. Magda had become my special protector, and because she enjoyed the respect of most other vendors they followed her example. By the time I did learn how to sell and became a real competitor, I was one of them, and they saw me not as an intruder but as a friend.

I was an eager student and soon learned a number of useful tricks. It was best to put the most beautiful rolls on the top of the basket and leave the ugly ones at the bottom. When handing over rolls to a buyer one had to reach quickly to the bottom layers and so dispose of hard-to-sell items first. To accomplish this one had to move quickly, and at the same time distract the customer by talking about something quite different from the business at hand. Whenever someone inquired about the price, it was best to pretend not to have heard the question and instead to praise the quality of the goods. When the question was repeated, the answer had to be given quickly and casually, as if one were offering a bargain: "Oh, only one zloty." After mentioning the price one resumed talking about the high quality of the goods, and then asked a matter-of-fact question about the amount the customer wanted to buy. Throughout the transaction one had not only to behave as if the customer was eager to buy, but also actually to believe it. To be sure, one also had to be flexible. Some customers resented too much talk or were put off by the approach, so it was important to read small clues. It was also important to remember faces. Customers liked to be recognized—it made them feel special—and it was smart to treat anyone who came twice as a devoted and faithful client.

As my selling skills improved, so did our business. With increased volume and more practice, my mother's skills improved too. Her rolls became more attractive and therefore easier to sell, and in time we acquired steady customers who came back to buy only our rolls.

For awhile I even had beginner's luck in the matter of raids. Magda had tried to prepare me for such an eventuality, explaining that a raid rarely came as a total surprise, so there was usually time to run and hide. Of course we all had to be constantly alert to any signs of approaching danger, but Magda insisted that if I didn't lose my head I would not be caught. "Just run into any courtyard, knock on any door, and people will let you in," she said.

She was right. Poles were eager to help one another when the Nazis threatened, here in the marketplace as elsewhere. When the Nazis tried to round up sellers, they did not bother to search in private homes, contenting themselves with catching those who could not or did not run away.

For many weeks after I started working there the Nazis left the market alone. When, for the first time, the word "raid" ran through the crowd, I was fortunate to be close to Magda. She gave me one significant look and yelled, "Run after me." Considering her weight, I was amazed at how fast she moved. I could hardly keep up with her and was quickly out of breath, but fear made me follow her blindly. I did not talk, I did not think, I did not bother about the rolls that fell out of our baskets. I only kept my eyes on my friend and ran wherever she did, bumping into other people or being bumped into, noticing no more than they did. There was no time to be polite; there was no time to be angry. In this frantic dash for safety, though the sellers ran in all different directions, we were united against the common enemy.

Soon Magda and I were in a courtyard. A door opened, someone pulled us in, we were safe.

I had thought Magda and I had run faster than

anybody else, but two other sellers were there before us. We sat around the kitchen table and talked about the raid. Each of the adults had a different version of how the raid had started, how many Germans there might be, what goods were likely to be confiscated, and so forth. They chatted on in a matter-of-fact way, as if the raid really didn't concern them at all. I was still scared and shaken, and could not even collect my thoughts. I sat there wondering at the composure of the others.

After a surprisingly short time, without any fuss, they decided it would be safe to go back, and we resumed our places in the market. Looking at all the restored bustle and listening to the animated voices, I found it hard to remember the frantic spectacle the market had presented less than an hour before.

Later I understood that the sellers I'd hidden with were used to raids, that raids were part of their work and nothing to be excited about. Later, I too became less emotional about them. Taking a more relaxed view of raids made our work easier. Fear could be paralyzing, so to stay in the black market one had to be fearless, though one also had to be alert.

This was the very principle my family and I had to live by. "Fear," my father had said, "is a luxury we cannot afford. We must be cautious, but we must not be fearful." And as we followed his precepts we tried hard to give to our lives some semblance of normality. We tried desperately not to indulge in gloomy thoughts. We tried to plan ahead, pretending and believing that life would continue to move along relatively uneventfully until the end of the war.

Christmas was approaching. It was a joyous holiday, with special emphasis on the religious celebration, relaxation, and food. Small misunderstandings were forgotten, people were expected to be more charitable, and no matter how poor families were, they ate well on Christmas. Some would go for weeks without extras to be able to feast on Christmas.

In the true spirit of the holiday, the Homars made us a part of their celebration. Their natural, casual way helped to make us glad to join them. The excitement, the anticipation of good things to come, did give life a semblance of normality. I felt strongly that I was a part of my surroundings, I almost forgot who I really was.

The second room was to become the center for the celebration, and because space was limited we decided to hang the Christmas tree from the ceiling above the table. Trees themselves were inexpensive, but decorations were costly and hard to get, so we had to limit ourselves to homemade ornaments. We collected a great store of wrapping paper, bows, little pieces of wood, thread, and boxes. My sister became a major supplier of discarded silver foil wrappings, colorful string, and ribbons, luxuries available only to the Nazis. We transformed these materials into a variety of ornaments. Stefa was particularly deft and inventive, the real artist among us, and I was happy to assist her. The two of us had a fine time sitting at the kitchen table trying to think of one more variation on the basic theme, one more combination of materials. The results were impressive, and they had cost us nothing. We had a beautifully decorated tree of which we were all proud.

We were all excited as we planned and helped prepare the food. My mother was busy baking cakes, this time for our own use. The rest of us cooked all kinds of things, but most notably, in a big cast-iron pot, the national Polish dish called bigos, which consists of different pork meats, sausages, and sauerkraut, served alone or with boiled potatoes.

On Christmas Eve, traditionally the most festive time in the holiday season, Stefa, Basia, Wojtek, Helena, my sister, my parents, and I all dressed up, gathered around our beautifully decorated table, and sang Christmas carols. The custom was to have an uneven number of courses, so our dinner was a truly memorable feast of eleven dishes. Whatever differences there may have been among us seemed to blur and dissolve in the warm atmosphere of this Christmas Eve.

That night the Nazis lifted the curfew. Stefa invited me to join them for a midnight mass, and when I hesitated my parents urged me to go. "Danka and Wojtek are staying home. They will give us enough protection," my mother said. I was anxious to go, but looked first at my sister to see if she did not mind staying behind. She smiled and nodded her approval.

On the way to the services, Stefa put her arm around me to protect me from the cold. On the other side of me Helena did the same, asking gently, "Krysia, are you cold? Let me give you my shawl."

Their attention comforted me. So did the atmosphere inside the church. There was something uplifting in the service and in the emotions I sensed around me. I felt very much a part of the church and of the Homars. I felt inspired.

When the service was over we went out into a freezing, starry night. A full moon cast its brilliant bluish light and created strange shadows on the ground, which was covered with a crisp, grayish frost. The air was cold and clean. Our breath turned into steam, forming indefinite and mysterious clouds that briefly floated in the moonlight and then disappeared into nowhere. None of us felt like talking. We moved quietly, arms around each other, and the only sound was the occasional faint squeak of our feet when they touched the frost on the ground. The pressure of our arms expressed all we could have said. A memorable day ended with a memorable night.

Christmas created a special bond between our two families, but we had been getting along surprisingly well even before that. To be sure, my family made

every effort not to offend or antagonize the Homars.
Quite apart from that, the Homars made things easy
for us. In our day-to-day contact they never took
advantage of us, they never behaved cruelly or even
inconsiderately, but treated us instead with respect
and kindness. Especially after we moved away from
Tadek and Ziutka, Stefa set the tone for our relationship. She was a kind, peace-loving person, who
never raised her voice or seemed to disagree with
anyone. Instead, she could not stand conflict and
when a minor misunderstanding arose she tried to
gloss it over.

Considering our close quarters and the dangerous
times, this was a real blessing. I often heard my
parents say we were fortunate to have come across
such considerate people.

As a successful seller I had little time left for the
children, whom I could see only on my way home
from short days at the market. Even then my time
was limited, and I could not be of any great help. I
was distressed that they were so neglected. Although
Stefa tried to act as my substitute, her visits were
sporadic, and particularly in cold weather she preferred to stay home. More often than not, the children were left to their own devices.

Fortunately, Jadwiga, who was barely three, was
becoming independent and resourceful. In self-
defense she had learned how to dress and feed herself and was also capable of dressing and feeding her
brother. I did what I could to encourage her. During
my brief visits I tried to instill in her a sense of
responsibility for Waldek. Sometimes I did it by brib-
ing her with rolls and candy, sometimes by flattery,
sometimes by combining the two techniques. I did
not care how I did it, as long as Waldek got at least
some of the attention he needed.

Brother and sister were very different. When I
gave Jadwiga a roll she never offered to share it with

Waldek, and when I made her share she somehow always managed to get the bigger part. If I offered Waldek a candy or a roll he would always ask, *"And for Adzia"* (For Jadwiga). Sometimes I tried to give him a special treat which he need not share with anyone, but I never succeeded. He refused to eat even one small candy by himself. He always saved a part for his sister. And whenever I divided anything between them, Waldek would invariably reach for the smaller share. He loved his sister without reservation. Jadwiga loved him in a more selfish and limited way. But there was no one else who would assume any responsibility for Waldek, so I was grateful for her help. I was grateful for any help.

Our business continued to expand and our rolls steadily became more popular. My mother was imaginative and liked to try out new methods. She added potatoes to some dough, which reduced the cost without affecting the quality. One of her special secrets was to add a little sugar to all the dough to improve the taste. To the first simple rolls we eventually added sweet rolls, rolls filled with jam, and rolls of different shapes and sizes. My steady customers began praising the excellence of our baked goods.

One day, though, the praise alarmed me. After biting into a roll, a man who bought from me regularly said, "These rolls are delicious. They taste like Jewish challah." I could think of nothing to say to him. I was upset. When I told my parents, they worried too, and urged me to watch this particular customer carefully. All I noticed was that he continued to buy and eat our rolls with relish, and never mentioned their Jewish qualities again. It took us some time to accept the fact that his remark had been made in all innocence and that no hostile action would follow.

After I became well established in the marketplace,

I discovered that some of my co-workers were smuggling in farm products. They went to the country by train and bought meats, sausages, and cheeses, which they then sold at a profit to local stores. Eventually they invited me to join them, assuring me that the risks were minimal. In the event of a raid they could always pretend that the merchandise was not theirs, so losing it was the worst that could happen. Eager to earn additional money, I agreed to join them.

The best time for such a trip was one of the slow market days, when all activities ended around two or so. This meant that we could be back with our purchases between five and six. We were virtually assured of selling whatever we bought. On the train we gossiped, joked, and sang, and once we had arrived at our destination, we went together from one peasant hut to another, bargaining as a group, devising new ways to get the best deal possible and forever tasting all the delicacies. Most of us looked upon these excursions as diversions, and as a way of outwitting the Nazis. The profits were not spectacular. Too many people had the same idea, and the competition was fierce.

My career as a smuggler was shortlived, however, because our baking business soon claimed all my attention. With time I had come to realize that some of the bakers no longer came to the market. Instead, they supplied all their goods to stores. Although the stores paid lower prices the sales volume was bigger, and because all orders were placed in advance there was never any waste. I passed this information on to my parents. They liked the idea, and decided that we should try to establish a wholesale business, which would surely be less strenuous for me and in the end more profitable.

To begin with, on slow market days I went to several stores and tried to sell them our rolls. At first they were cautious because they wanted to see if their customers would like our product, and their orders were modest. Nonetheless, I stopped at all these stores each day before I reached the market to deliver the orders. This meant that I had to get up earlier than usual and that by the end of the day I was more tired. But it was only a temporary arrangement. If it did not prove feasible to go into the wholesale business, I would return to selling only in the market.

Gradually both the number of stores and the size of the orders increased, and I became an established supplier to eight. Without exception they were all black-market operations, carried out in private homes and selling a wide variety of goods. I had to cut back on my time in open market, and then stopped altogether. I went there only to shop or to pay a visit to my old friends.

The stores I supplied also sold bootleg vodka. I suggested to my parents that I could sell them Tadek's vodka as well as the rolls, and so increase our earnings without much extra effort. My parents went along with my suggestion. I was limited by the weight I could carry and never sold more than two or three bottles of vodka a day. Still, I was delighted with the additional income it brought in.

No matter what the season or the weather, I had to get up at four and leave the house at five. My customers were scattered over a wide area, and my working day involved a three-hour walk. Far more than just walking was involved, however. In each store I had to spend time settling accounts and taking orders for the next day, and I wrote everything down clearly in accordance with explicit instructions from my father. After a few initial mistakes the whole process moved smoothly. I soon came to welcome these stops, which gave me a chance to sit down, rest, and even have a snack.

As she had done from the start, my mother always packed a number of scorched or misshapen rolls for my own use. To me they were a great delicacy. But no matter how many of them I ate I was never full, and I could not comprehend how people could satisfy their hunger with rolls or white bread alone.

An expanded business meant that I had to carry a heavier load, which consisted of rolls made from more than sixty pounds of flour. Despite my size I felt very strong. My acceptance of the job was total, and it did not occur to me that I might not be able to carry the load, no matter how heavy it became. But because I was so small, we had to devise a system for balancing the baskets properly. I carried a basket on each arm, and the third hung from my two clenched hands held in front of me. This way the weight was more or less equally distributed. The size of the baskets made me almost invisible.

When I left the house during the winter months it was still night. As I was ready to go, surrounded by the three big, heavy baskets, my mother, tired from a whole night's work, would see me to the door. She had a sad and loving look on her face as she kissed me good-bye. I preferred not to look at her because there was something about her sadness that made me want to cry. Each time I forced myself to smile, hoping to cheer her up. I never waited to see if I had succeeded. I could not face her pain, exhaustion, and resignation.

I knew that my mother stood in the cold little anteroom and kept looking through the chinks between the planks until I disappeared from view. I felt her sad eyes on me. I knew her well enough to know that she cried, and I had to suppress an urge to cry myself.

My sadness had nothing to do with me. I felt sorry for my mother, not for myself. I would have loved to convince her that what I was doing was easy for me. I often had an urge to turn around, go back, and tell her so. I never did, because I knew that she would deny her feelings. We had an unspoken understanding never to complain to each other.

When I returned, my mother would be asleep. She slept only during the day. Her nights she spent baking. It was no small accomplishment to transform fifty or sixty pounds of flour into rolls, night after night. My father tried to assist her by setting up the scales and weighing the flour and other ingredients, and by laying out all the necessary utensils. The actual making of the dough, the shaping, and the baking, she had to do herself. There was plenty of time to prepare a fresh batch of rolls while an earlier one was baking. We had only one oven, and that was precisely the reason my mother had to be up all night, most of the time on her feet.

I frequently noticed her swollen legs, but when I expressed concern, she laughed. In those days my mother never complained about her health, even though she had reason to. Neither exhaustion nor a sore throat, not even a fever, kept her from doing her job. Even so, it was fortunate that throughout the whole period neither of my parents became seriously ill. To have called a doctor would have been out of the question. How could a doctor be asked to see someone who did not exist?

We worked hard, helping one another as much as we could, without complaining. And we were satisfied with our business. Our share of the profits fed the entire household, which meant that we did not have to touch whatever little jewelry and gold we still had. Every day when I returned my father greeted me with a satisfied smile, and then the two of us would move to the next room, where we counted the money and checked to see if it tallied with my sales. That done, we would go over the orders for the next day, and decide on the amount of flour, yeast, food coloring, and other ingredients needed. My father never tired of emphasizing how important this business was. "Just imagine, if it were not for our bakery we might not have survived. At least our financial worries are taken care of." His satisfaction and approval made me forget my exhaustion, and I often wondered if he knew how beneficial his comments were to me.

We had started the business because we needed money, but looking at my father, so absorbed in the bookkeeping and planning, and listening to my mother breathing in the deep satisfied sleep of exhaustion, I often realized that our business gave us more than one kind of return.

Besides relieving us from serious financial worries, our bakery was a blessing in other ways. It made time pass faster for my parents, who now found their endless confinement inside one cramped house easier to bear. My father had suffered more than my mother from the monotony, and the baking business gave his abilities a new outlet. He was manager, president, and assistant baker, all in one. In a half joking, half serious way, he devised ingenious ways for making larger profits.

Throughout the war he never lost his optimism or the sense of humor that enabled him to laugh at himself. As a realist he must have had his doubts about our chances for survival. He took care never to express them. On the other hand, he never minimized the dangers. Sometimes, when we were alone, I would ask him how he saw our future, and his answer was always the same: "We will make it, if we are careful. We *must* make it, and we *must* be cautious."

It was reassuring to hear him say that. His strength and courage were contagious, and served as an inspiration to the rest of us.

As soon as it became obvious that the baking would take all night, we had suggested to Helena that she'd sleep better if she moved her bed into the next room. She refused, insisting that neither the noise nor the light disturbed her. Indeed, she really did seem able to sleep through all the bustle and clatter. She was remarkably hardy and her repeated assertions that she was never ill were borne out. Even when some of us had sore throats and fever she somehow managed to stay healthy. For her, being ill was an act of weakness, a giving up.

One day, however, she awoke with a strange cough. When the rest of us urged her to stay in bed, she became angry and left the house as usual. She returned from work in a bad mood and refused to talk to us. Next morning, when she tried to get up her body disobeyed. At first we thought she was angry with us for urging her to stay home. We soon understood that she was angry at herself. It was as if she could not forgive herself for being sick. She resented the fact that her body dared not do what she wanted it to do.

Because Helena's bed was still in the kitchen, it was easy for my parents to become invisible—"non-existent"—when the doctor visited her. Despite his ministrations, it became obvious that she was failing rapidly. She seemed to dwindle in front of our eyes. She must have come to realize that she was nearing the end, because she gave up fighting. But her valiant spirit and innate courage were as manifest as ever.

Soon she started talking about her impending death with a sort of detached clarity devoid of self-pity, and if any of us ventured to disagree with her she became angry. True to herself, on her deathbed as in life, she hated any kind of pretense. She was conscious, and she was in command of the situation. First she asked for a priest, and after he left she told us to come close to her bed so she could say good-bye to us all. One by one we did so, and most of us were crying. Weak though she was, she still managed to disapprove. "What is the point of crying?" she demanded. "We all have to die!"

When Ziutka's turn came, Helena turned her face away to the wall, and with an angry motion made it clear that she should leave. Whatever Ziutka had been guilty of, Helena refused to forgive her. Then Helena asked, almost inaudibly, for Stefa. There was the suggestion of a gentle amused smile on her face as she whispered, "Stefa, you were better to me than I deserved. All I have is in the mattress. It is for you. Thank you." With the same expression on her face, she closed her eyes and died. She died simply, without fuss, just as she had lived.

We all mourned for her, each of us in a different way, but all of us more deeply than we would have expected. Selfish, self-centered Ziutka was truly shaken by the death of this old woman. It was understandable that Stefa should take the death of her formidable mother-in-law so much to heart. She often gave way to tears, and in her deep depression lost her appetite. Fearing for her health, we coaxed her to eat.

Even Czarus, our watch dog, seemed heartbroken. To stop him from howling, Wojtek released him from his kennel when Helena's body had been removed, and let him into the kitchen. He made straight for the bed, jumped upon the mattress and began to sniff at it, whimpering in a way that sounded almost like a human cry, full of pain and sorrow.

All of us knew we would go on missing Helena. But in the meantime her death created problems that had to be dealt with right away. As a Catholic, she had to be buried on the third day after her death, and between death and burial, in accordance with tradition, the body should have rested either in a special chapel attached to the church or in our best room, prepared for burial and surrounded by candles and flowers. During this period visitors were expected to come to pay their respects, and refreshments were served. The use of the chapel was costly, and within our circle it was an unheard-of extravagance. But if Helena's body had been placed in the second room, my parents would have had to stay in their hiding place throughout the coming and going of the visitors, creating an impossible situation with the cramped space, the dampness, and my father's cough. As a solution, my parents offered to pay for the use of the chapel. And so Helena the beggar left the world in greater style than she could have imagined. And to think that Jews had made this possible!

Life had to go on, and my father believed that there was no point in dwelling on sad events. Hoping to help Stefa out of her depression, he urged her to become involved again in the life around her. Her son's family, he pointed out, really needed her help. And Stefa, who respected my father, began to visit Tadek's household far more regularly. Taking care of her grandchildren and helping with the housework that Ziutka found so tiresome helped Stefa overcome her sense of loss.

Although we all listened to my father's suggestions, the amount of influence he had over the Homars amazed me. After all, we were dependent on them, in a real sense at their mercy. And yet they sought his advice, and listened to his suggestions with respect.

Even though he was very much in control of our household, much in our situation was beyond my father's control. No matter how many precautions we took, the possibility of sudden disaster was a constant, hovering presence. We were essentially powerless, and we had no way of anticipating events either good or bad, major or minor.

As a rule, when I returned from making my deliveries, I would let myself into the apartment with a key. One day, as I was taking the key out of the lock and about to step inside, I felt a heavy hand on my shoulder. I turned around and found myself face to face with a German soldier. I had not heard any footsteps. He must have been following me very closely, so closely that Czarus, who ordinarily barked loudly at any approaching stranger, had considered him a friend. Now the soldier stood close and grinned down at me in an oddly questioning, almost sheepish way.

Before I had time to collect my thoughts, both of us were inside the kitchen. It was empty. My parents were in the second room. I had to warn them. But how? Though my German was virtually nonexistent, I began to use it as loudly as I could, chattering with no idea what I was trying to say.

The soldier muttered something. At first I was too nervous to grasp any words at all, but then it dawned on me that he was saying, over and over again, *"Mädchen, Mädchen."* He was looking for girls. Luckily for me my looks did not qualify me as a *"Mädchen."* As he talked, he moved to the door leading to the next room. I continued to talk, loudly and nervously, hoping to prevent him from going into the room, hoping to give my parents time to hide.

The German entered the second room. As if in a trance, I followed. My father emerged from behind the door. My mother was sound asleep. The German took one step backward, but then stopped and for a second the two men stared at each other. My father, with his gray-blue eyes, coldly watched the German. Faced with that penetrating look, he became ill at ease. From the start there had been nothing belligerent about him, and now, hesitantly and uncomfortably, he asked about the availability of girls. Nodding, but still not taking his eyes off him, my father pointed to the window, suggesting some routes with his hand. Relieved, with a timid smile and a brief thank you, the soldier left abruptly.

Belatedly, Czarus began to bark. My mother slept on. She had been spared the terror that my father, for all his seeming calm, had shared with me.

The incident emphasized the precariousness of our position, and it was followed by a number of Nazi raids. Even so, we went on being miraculously fortunate. My parents' hiding place was passing the test, because so far it had not occurred to any of the Nazi searchers to move the old valise and scrutinize the floor. My father's cough was an ever-present danger, but this too had no disastrous consequences. To some extent the smallness of the apartment was responsible for our good luck. Searching the whole place did not take more than five minutes, and my father was usually able to refrain from coughing for about ten minutes at a time.

On one occasion, however, after a thorough and unsuccessful search throughout the neighborhood, the Nazis returned to our place. This time they came to feast on pork and wine that they had discovered by chance in our landlord's apartment. They must have been in a mellow mood, and instead of persecuting the landlord they merely confiscated his hoard of food and drink.

They selected Stefa to be their cook. As soon as they had given her instructions, they moved to the room whose floor hid my parents. They placed themselves around the table as Stefa and I looked on in horror and disbelief. Amid laughter, singing, and clinking glasses, they kept urging us to action. "*Schnell, schnell!*"

We needed no urging. Once the initial shock was over we worked at lightning speed. Never before had I seen poor, inefficient Stefa move so fast. As I kept rapidly cutting and frying the meat I hardly knew what I was doing. We were not even remotely tempted to sample the rare delicacies we were preparing for the Nazis. I could only think of my father's cough, and I was all ears. Then, as a nervous reaction, I myself began to cough. Stefa looked at me in amazement, but she did not utter a word, and no one else paid any attention to me.

As the Germans continued to drink and eat they became more noisy and more boisterous. I served them with the most zealous efficiency, simultaneously straining my ears, but except for the clamor of their animated talk and laughter, I could hear nothing. Only one question kept running through my head: Would they ever leave? Once again, time seemed to have reached a standstill. Finally, still noisy and jovial, the Germans departed, followed by loud barks from Czarus.

After my parents emerged from their hiding place, my mother told us that my father had indeed had a coughing attack. "His cough will send me to my grave!" she said. We were too stunned to say anything. The Germans' own clamor had saved my parents.

Peace did not last long. One day, as I reached my last customer, he told me that another storekeeper I dealt with had been denounced. His store had been raided and all the goods confiscated, among them our rolls and vodka. Because the Nazis were interested in tracing the source of the bootlegged vodka, the owner had been severely beaten, and he had given them my name and address. "Right now," my informant said, "the Nazis are on their way to your house."

For a moment I was paralyzed by the possibility of disaster. But then I knew that I had to get there before the Nazis. My parents had to be hidden, the valise had to be placed over their hiding place, and all the evidence of vodka and our baking operations had to be swept out of sight! The road was long and I had no time to lose. Knowing that this was a matter of life and death gave me extraordinary strength. I ran and ran, propelled by fear. The closer I came to our place the faster I ran.

By the time I reached our courtyard I felt as though I myself was already dead. All was quiet. I burst into our apartment. Explanations had to be kept to a minimum, and we had no time even to feel frightened. As my parents slipped into their hiding place, my father called out, "You must not let them take you, go and hide too." And as I was about to cover their hole, he added, "Go away, but do not go to Ziutka's. Stay away from apartments."

My parents had never wanted me to join them in their hiding place, fearing that in case of discovery I would be treated like a Jew. It was safer to be caught as a Pole.

I knew that I had to leave, but before I left I had to help Stefa conceal all the evidence. Our neighbors were most helpful, and allowed us to store with them all the equipment and materials for both our businesses. Within minutes, all was clear. Stefa cried as I hugged her good-bye. "Be careful," she murmured. She stayed on, waiting for the Germans.

This took place on a beautiful summer day in 1944. I went out into the fields beyond the house, where the grass and wheat had grown tall enough to hide me completely. There I remained, watching and listening and imagining. I became too nervous to stay in one place and started to roam the fields, making sure that no one saw me. I had no idea what was happening. I could not shake off visions of total disaster. I felt tired, tired of struggling, and more alone than ever. I was pulled in opposite directions by two powerful forces. I wanted to come out and I did not want to, I wanted to know what the Germans were doing and I preferred not to know. A paralyzing fear kept me in the fields until dusk. Only then did I come out cautiously and slowly. Instead of going home I went to our neighbors. They, of course, were aware only of our black-market operations and nothing else. When they told me that all was well, I had a hard time believing them. It sounded too good to be true.

When I did go home, I learned that the Nazis had

arrived right after I left. As they searched the house they kept asking where the smuggler of vodka was. At first Stefa pretended not to know what they meant. Then she explained that I was a little girl, and probably out playing with other children in the neighborhood. They questioned her about the vodka. She insisted they must have been misinformed, and denied that I could have had anything to do with it. She even showed them my birth certificate. The Nazis were not satisfied and took Stefa to the Gestapo headquarters. There a succession of Nazis interrogated her. In different ways they all asked her about me and my black-market operations. As they questioned her they beat her on the head and shoulders and arms with their fists and rubber truncheons. They threatened to kill her unless she told the truth. Stefa refused to change or elaborate on her story. I was a little girl, they had been misinformed, they were making a terrible mistake.

After about three hours of interrogation, threats, and beatings, they released Stefa. She came home with her head, arms, and shoulders covered with cuts and bruises. As we tended to her injuries, she smiled. "I did fool them!" she said. "Didn't I fool them?"

We agreed. Not only had she fooled the Nazis, she had fooled us. Because of her mild self-effacing manner we had thought of her as a coward. Her resistance and presence of mind seemed out of character. In adversity she had drawn upon unsuspected resources of courage and had saved us all.

Surprisingly, and for unfathomable reasons, the Nazis never tried to check what Stefa had told them. Whether they believed her or became indifferent to what after all had been a small-scale operation, they did not come looking for me.

Tadek, possibly feeling safe because the Nazis had not raided his place, continued with his bootleg operations, but I gave up my minor part in them and devoted all my energies to our bakery.

Soon life resumed its usual course and once again we refused to dwell on the past. After each new shock or narrow escape, we went on as before. We continued to hope.

CHAPTER EIGHT

◄►►

And Now?

LATE summer of 1944 brought encouraging news
about German losses and retreats. It came, of course,
only through unofficial or illegal channels, and people told and retold the news to each other with great
enthusiasm and high hopes. My customers became
my main source of information. Each morning, as I
went from store to store, I listened to them talk
about what was happening both locally and on the
front, and tried hard to remember everything they
said. My father counted on such information, and I
hated to disappoint him. He had begun to greet me
every time I returned with "What good news do you
have for me today?" And whenever I had a new Nazi
defeat to report, it was as if we all had shared a
personal victory.

The Germans were not only retreating at the front,
they were also losing the battle against the Polish
underground, which had intensified its sabotage operations. The burning of bridges, the blowing up of
important military installations, and the killing of
key Nazi officials eventually became daily events.
Members of the underground as a rule managed to
disappear after an act of terrorism, and the frus-
trated Nazis avenged themselves on innocent civil-

ians. We heard of villages being burned to the ground for having harbored Polish or Russian partisans. Sometimes the Germans surrounded such villages and the trapped inhabitants were burned alive. Often, too, they set fire to entire forests in the hope of destroying underground hideouts. They acted with particular speed and fury after the death of one of their comrades, executing ten or more innocent Poles for every slain Nazi.

As the killing of Nazis became more frequent, so did the execution of Poles, until it was dangerous to walk the streets. In fact, whenever we knew that a German had lost his life we tried not to venture out until after retaliatory measures had taken place. We learned to identify various danger signs. If we were outside and saw other people beginning to run, we wasted no time in running for cover ourselves. More subtle signs of approaching danger, such as a certain indefinable tension in the air, became part of our daily lives. Even an unusual period of inactivity could mean that a storm was approaching. But all the warnings and signals were not enough, and the Germans continued to round up innocent civilians. The chances of survival for any one who was caught depended on how many victims the Nazis needed. They were very precise. Whatever ratio they decided upon—ten Poles, or twenty, for one Nazi killed—it had to be met.

At first such reprisals took place in the afternoon and in the central part of town, and for a while I felt safe when I was making my deliveries. But I could not stay home in the afternoons because it was then that Stefa and I had to buy our baking supplies. Sometimes, when Stefa was unavailable, I went out alone.

One beautiful summer day I was returning home alone with a few small purchases. I was engrossed in pleasant thoughts and unaware of my surroundings. Suddenly I felt a certain tension in the air, and stopped short. A moment later people began running frantically in all directions. I knew that, like them, I had to take refuge in a courtyard, and, like them, I began running wildly in search of one that the Nazis had not already taken over. I knew no one in the neighborhood, so I turned into the first "free" courtyard I came to. I knocked at a door just beyond the gate, breathlessly crying, "Help! Help!" Not one but three or four doors opened and I sprinted into the nearest, seeing in a flash that other runners were darting into other apartments. Everything happened quickly. A moment later all was quiet: no running, no knocks, no slamming doors.

My protector, a young woman, looked pale and distraught. "Oh, my God," she said. "Only yesterday they shot people right in front of this house." Then, as if to console me, she added with a sad smile, "You are safe now, they never bother to come in." From the outside no noises reached us. The silence dragged on. I strained my ears for sounds, and waited. I waited and waited. Time was playing its tricks on me again, standing still when I wanted it to move on.

The young woman and I looked at each other tentatively. Then, as if afraid to disturb the silence, she whispered, "Don't be frightened, it will be over soon."

Her whisper was followed almost immediately by a shot. Then there was another, and another after that, and more until I stopped counting. But each shot made me feel as if one of those bullets were going through me.

Finally, there was silence again. An oppressive silence. The Nazis must have finished their job. We said nothing, and we could not bring ourselves to look at each other.

Presently she said, "You'd better wait. The bodies will be left there for a while." I obeyed, oblivious to time and to everything around me. This could not be real. I could not imagine that out there people who had been alive a few minutes ago were now dead. I had seen many dead people before, and I knew what being dead meant. And yet I did not know. Each time I was confronted with death it was as if I had never seen it before. Death was not something I could get used to.

My thoughts turned to my parents. They must be worried about me. Playing my part as a Polish girl, I explained to the young woman, who had not even asked my name, that my aunt was waiting for me and that I had to go.

As on earlier occasions, I did not feel that I was lying. At the moment, and for a moment, I was convinced again that Stefa was my aunt. And, again as before, I felt an odd confusion of emotions—fear because I was losing touch with my real self, but a kind of pleasure too, because it was so easy to give up and become my newer, safe self. The young woman nodded, as if approving. I thanked her and left.

In the street all was quiet again. Eerily quiet. Only a few people who, like me, must have been anxious to get home, were visible. They were all walking fast. Like them, I had no time to lose.

Then, aghast, I stopped abruptly. On the sidewalk close to the houses, almost in a straight line, lay the bodies of the victims just as they had fallen. Some looked like bundles bent in half, others sprawled out flat, face up or face down. Most of them were surrounded by puddles of blood, thick, dark red, still oozing from their wounds. A few of the faces had horribly distorted expressions, but others were masks, with no expression at all. I thought I saw them move, I thought I saw them breathe. Their thick dark blood was definitely moving, out and away from their bodies, flowing toward me. I was filled with horror, horror and guilt. How had it happened that I was here and they were there? In self-defense, I averted my eyes. My legs began to tremble. I could not move. I felt as if these dead were pulling at me, refusing to let me go, and it took an extraordinary effort to fight off the wave of nausea that swept over me. I knew that I had to get away, that if I did not and gave in to the nausea, something terrible would happen.

With what seemed a superhuman effort, I started to run. Only as the distance between me and the dead lengthened did the tears start to pour out. I burst into our apartment, crying and gasping, "They killed them, they killed them!"

My mother lovingly put me to bed as my father looked on in distress. They did not ask any questions. There was no need. Still crying, I fell asleep with my parents sitting beside me.

I could not afford to brood over what had happened. None of us could. We all had to go on as before.

And then, another dimension of concern was added to my work. As the killing of some civilians continued, so did the rounding up of others for deportation to Germany as cheap labor. By now the Nazis' standards for qualified workers had grown far less exacting, and my age and size were no longer a protection. Eventually the raids, followed by death or deportation, became an almost daily occurrence at any time of the day or night, in any part of Kielce. My instinct for impending danger became so acute that I could almost feel and smell it.

I knew my route very well by now, and when it became necessary I could easily slip into a ditch with my baskets either empty or full. Sometimes a customer would hide me. When a raid found me at home my parents always insisted that I hide with the other Polish children, and not with them. All the children in our compound hid in an old rundown barn whose main floor housed a cow and a goat. The loft, which was filled with hay, could be reached by placing a ladder against an opening in the ceiling.

There was enough hay to cover all of us, and as soon as we were safely hidden some adult down below would remove the ladder. One day we had barely scrambled into the loft when we heard the approaching sound of German voices. The old woman who was helping us busied herself with the animals. She had no choice but to leave the ladder in place. Leaning there against the opening to the loft, it served as an invitation to climb. In a moment we heard heavy footsteps coming up the ladder. "This is the end," I thought. I began to sweat. I dared not breathe. My heart was pounding loudly and violently, and I was sure the Nazis could hear it. The pounding grew louder as the steps came steadily closer.

Dizzy with terror, I realized that something was touching me. I did not move. A rifle was poking through the hay at my ribs. I waited for the inevitable, but the inevitable did not happen. After dreadful moments had passed, I heard the footsteps descending the ladder.

Later, a number of us agreed that we had been poked with a rifle. The incident deeply disturbed my parents. My mother was particularly concerned. She insisted that the barn loft was too exposed. She tried to convince my father that in future raids I should hide under the floor with them. But my father would not hear of it. "She is not going to be caught with us," he said. When he reached a decision, no one could argue with him.

All through the rapidly changing situation our baking business continued to relieve us of acute financial worry. Tadek, despite his inefficiency and his sporadic drinking, was less dependent on our support than he had been, and although he and Ziutka were never able to save a penny, they were content with their economic situation. Whenever the discussion turned to business, they both emphasized that they enjoyed being financially independent.

Our lives, however, were always in danger. It could come from any direction. Late one afternoon Ziutka rushed into our apartment, crying, "We are lost, we are lost!" She told us that she had come directly from a meeting with Teresa, the friend who had been the mistress of a succession of Nazi officials. She had warned Ziutka that the Germans knew the Homars were protecting Jews. They intended to act on the information that very night. Convinced that we were here and that we must have a hiding place in the apartment, they planned to tear up the entire place.

Ziutka insisted that to avoid disaster we had to leave right away. We should not even wait for my sister to return from work, we should go get her. As she spoke, Ziutka became increasingly agitated. Her voice grew louder and more insistent. She kept wringing her hands as she repeated: "You must leave at once! At once!"

Stefa nodded in agreement. Then, visibly moved, she began in a quiet resigned way to cry.

My mother, dry-eyed, said in a bewildered, automatic manner, over and over again, "Where shall we go? Where can we go? What will happen?" I had difficulty grasping the situation. I heard what was said but was too stunned to comprehend the reality behind the words. I looked to my father for help.

At the moment he sat there passively, without uttering a word. Only those who really knew him could tell that he was engrossed in thought. His forehead was full of deep, deep wrinkles, and his eyes intently watched Ziutka's face. When she had finished, he asked quietly and gently, still keeping his eyes on her, "How do the Germans know all this? How did they find out?"

For a split second Ziutka hesitated. Then she said that one of the neighbors had been spying on us and had given all the evidence to the Nazis. She did not know exactly how the neighbor had done that. "After all," she added, "it was my duty to come and warn you, not to wait for detailed information!" She continued by saying that we were fortunate that it was summer. She was still talking about the importance of good weather and how it would help us to hide, when to our surprise my father asked her to join him in the other room.

"Should I prepare some food for you?" we heard poor, weepy Stefa ask. Neither my mother nor I answered. Bewildered, we watched my father and Ziutka disappear into the next room and shut the door behind them. I sat dry-eyed, puzzled, lost in confused, contradictory emotions and thoughts. Where would we go? Who would take us? And what could my father be talking to Ziutka about?

No sound reached us, but when they reappeared, Ziutka looked more composed. My father wore an impassive, expressionless look. I knew that he was forcing himself not to show his feelings.

Then, still looking impassive, he made a matter-of-fact announcement: "Ziutka and I have decided that we should stay and try to overcome the danger together. We both feel that it will be safer this way for all of us."

My mother, Stefa, and I were all at a loss. A great weight was lifted from my soul. It was marvelous to know that we did not have to run and be killed. So great was the relief that I was unconcerned about the expected Nazi visit.

But the Nazis failed to come. They did not appear that night, or for a number of nights thereafter. In connection with this incident, indeed, they never came at all.

Secretly, and only to us, my father explained the entire episode. He had guessed—and subsequent events proved him right—that Ziutka had made up the story, and had shared the idea only with Tadek. Now that she saw herself as rich and financially independent she felt that we were superfluous, and wanted to be rid of us and the danger our presence entailed.

When we pressed him to elaborate, my father explained, "Once I felt sure that she was lying, I had to be very careful. I could not let her see that I understood what she was doing. To have her lose face would have been very dangerous." He had begun by agreeing with Ziutka that the most logical solution would be for us to leave. And yet, he pointed out, this would not avert the Homars' danger. Surely we were bound to be caught very soon, and when we were caught the Nazis would insist on knowing where we had been hiding. He was convinced that even under torture he and my mother would not tell about the Homars, but obviously he could not expect the same resistance from my sister and me. And when they knew about the Homars' protection of Jews, the Nazis would take action against them.

And so, because our leaving would not avert disaster, it might be wiser not to do a thing, and simply wait. A possibility existed, even though it was a slight one, that Teresa's information was exaggerated. It was possible, too, that the Nazis might be distracted by more pressing business. In any case, by leaving we all gained nothing and lost a lot, my father had told Ziutka. By staying, we might gain something.

In effect, my father was trying to convey to Ziutka the idea that by getting rid of us now she would not free herself from danger, but on the contrary would surely invite disaster. Ziutka was shrewd enough to understand the message. She may even have realized that my father saw through her scheme. We never found out whether she did or not.

When in my confusion I kept asking my father how Ziutka could have sent us to our death, he reminded me how self-centered she was. "She was only thinking about her own safety," he said. "She is incapable of thinking about others."

But his explanation still left me at a loss. I had

believed that she liked us, and I was sure she admired my father. I recalled how she sought his advice and followed it scrupulously, how she often said that he understood her problems better than anyone else. Yet I had to conclude that my father was right. Ziutka was too involved with herself to realize fully that by sending us away she would be sending us to die.

She showed no signs of remorse. Only Tadek was decent enough to feel ashamed. For a long time he went out of his way to avoid us, and never again did he seem fully relaxed in our company. As for us, we had to pretend that nothing had happened, and went on living more or less as we had all along.

The summer and fall of 1944 were coming to an end. I did not look forward to the approaching cold weather. The heavy load I had to carry, the long walks I had to take, the constant watch for danger I had to keep, were bad enough in warm weather. It wasn't just that I suffered from the cold itself. It made me feel less safe. In the event of a raid it was harder for me to run because the many layers of clothes inhibited my movements. I knew my parents were upset because my work was so exhausting and beset with mounting dangers. But we all continued to practice a kind of pretense—a pretense that there was nothing to complain about, a pretense that there was no need for us to worry about one another.

I never complained to either parent about my burdens, and I was glad that they never told me how sorry they felt for me. If they had done so, I might have begun to feel sorry for myself. Keeping our true feelings to ourselves, never revealing to each other that we all knew how desperate our situation really was—all this helped us to endure.

In different and touching ways, both my parents tried to show me how much they valued my efforts. They often praised me, saying how well I carried out my work. They tried to reward me in more tangible ways too, my mother by putting a few extra rolls on the side of the basket for me to eat, my father by insisting from time to time that I buy myself a quarter of a pound of ham or bacon. Now that we were not so pressed for money we could afford such occasional extravagances. As a rule I would devour these delicacies immediately though I felt guilty about not sharing them with my family. My father reminded me that at home they would be divided among all of us, so that nobody would have more than a tiny scrap. By not sharing I had enough to do me some good, he said: I needed those occasional extras to keep up my strength. Whether they really helped or not I had no way of knowing. What I did know was that at the time they seemed to make absolutely no impression on my stomach. I had a limitless appetite. And when my father told me that after the war he would buy me so much ham and white bread that I wouldn't be able to eat it all, I listened in amazement and disbelief, as if he were telling me a fairy tale too beautiful to come true.

Cold weather did bring with it some compensations, most especially my second Christmas in Kielce. As we had the year before, we planned to hang a tree from the ceiling in our second room.

I started working on the decorations by the middle of December. This year Stefa complained of poor eyesight and could do very little. And we could not help thinking about Helena, and feeling sad she was gone. Despite these changes, though, I was in excellent spirits and full of anticipation. Because our financial situation was more secure than the year before, our cakes would be richer and our bigos would have more meat in it. The bustle of preparation and the day-by-day waiting were almost as enjoyable as the actual feast would be.

On Christmas Eve, Stefa, Basia, Wojtek, my parents, my sister and I all dressed up and gathered around the table, prepared to start the festivities by singing carols. But we had barely sat down when there was a violent knock on the door. For a moment we were stunned. Then Ziutka called out to us. As she came in we saw that she was in terrible condition. She had a coat on but no warm shoes, her head was bare, and her hair in disarray. Jadwiga was with her, tearful and terrified. Ziutka immediately gave way to uncontrollable crying. All her self-assurance, all her strength of character, seemed to have left her. Between her sobs she managed to tell us that Tadek had come home drunk, that he had beaten her and wrecked the apartment. Worst of all, he had seized little Waldek by the hair and had begun to slam his body against the bed. It was at that point that Ziutka had seized Jadwiga's hand and come running to us.

I was aghast. How could she have left Waldek with a raving maniac? How could she have thought only of saving herself, when her son was possibly being murdered? I was in a state of shock. My bewilderment began to give way to a strong feeling of contempt and hate for Ziutka. Then I caught my father's eye, and I understood that I had to hide my feelings. As calmly as I could, I agreed with Basia that she and I would go for Waldek. Ziutka told us about the clothes she wanted us to bring for her and the children, and in no time we were on our way.

As we neared the apartment we saw that all the lights were on and that the main door was ajar. For a moment we stood listening. When we heard nothing we entered cautiously. Broken glasses and china, broken chairs, and pots from the stove littered the floor. No one was in sight.

We moved on tiptoe into the next room. There too were broken chairs, mixed together with branches and ornaments ripped from the Christmas tree and with a tangled scatter of clothing. Then we heard loud snoring and saw Tadek. He was sprawled on the floor in a torn shirt and pants, with his head and arms and torso leaning against the edge of the bed. And Waldek was sitting in his own small bed. He did not make a sound. He stretched his arms in our direction. I started to cry as I moved toward him, but he put his finger to his mouth, warning me to silence. When I was close to him, I saw that his eyes were wide open and looked much bigger than I had ever seen them before. They were full of fright, and the enormous tears that came from them did not stop even after I held him in my arms.

I could not stop crying myself. I felt as if my heart would burst with the pain and love I felt for him. I squeezed him tight and he did not object. He continued to shed his brilliant, silent tears. The indescribable mixture of pain, sadness, resignation, and wisdom in his eyes touched me to the core.

As Basia and I ran around looking for clothes and then dressed Waldek, I felt happy that he was alive, sad and angry that he was suffering. All three of us continued to cry quietly as we finished our task and left the apartment. It was a very different Christmas from the one we had anticipated.

At home we discovered that Waldek's head was hurting, and that some of his hair was gone. No doubt this was where his father had held him when he hit him against the bed. Fortunately the wound itself proved to be superficial and healed without trouble.

For days Waldek behaved as if he were in shock. His eyes remained unusually big and frightened, even when his mouth smiled. But in the end it was clear that his overall disposition had changed very little. He was still an extraordinarily sweet little boy, with the same gentle and appealing personality.

Immediately after Christmas, Ziutka left for Otwock to stay with her parents, taking Jadwiga with her. She told us that if Tadek wanted them back he would have to come for them. Strangely enough, even though she loved Waldek more than she did

Jadwiga, she left him with us. Her departure was meant as a punishment for Tadek. She was convinced that he would miss his favorite, Jadwiga, and would come to humble himself before his wife.

We were delighted to have Waldek with us. We showered him with love and attention and indulged him in every way we could. Tadek began to come to our place more and more often, and to take greater interest in his son than he ever had before. As a result, father and son drew closer. All in all, Tadek seemed like a man entirely satisfied with himself and his life. He showed no inclination whatsoever to see Ziutka and Jadwiga.

Soon letters from Ziutka began to arrive, asking us when Tadek would be coming for them. But Tadek was getting along surprisingly well, and he paid no attention. Finally Ziutka wrote to my father and asked him to intercede for her. For once my father's efforts produced few results. Tadek said that as far as he was concerned she need not bother to come back, but if she wanted to and did it on her own, he would accept her back. That was the best offer she could ever hope for, he told my father, and he seemed to mean it. The end result was that on a wintry day a somewhat dejected Ziutka and Jadwiga arrived in our apartment, and the family was reunited.

Now, however, Tadek's bootlegging business began to suffer. His profits were shrinking to such a point that he needed financial assistance. It was hard to know whether this was due to excessive competition or his inefficiency or both. Whatever the reason, it meant that we had to supplement his income. Fortunately we could afford to do so, and when it became clear that Tadek's business was not going to improve, my father suggested that if Stefa consented he was ready to divide the baking profits three ways. Good-natured and generous Stefa promptly agreed. Even with this change there was enough for all of us.

My parents were well satisfied. Especially after

Ziutka's attempt to be rid of us, it was safer to have that part of the Homar family dependent on us as well.

In fact, we were so pleased with the arrangement that my father refrained from advising Tadek how to improve his bootlegging business. When Tadek asked my father for a course of action, he became a master of double-talk. I had a hard time suppressing a smile as I listened to him prefacing each of his suggestions with a serious and grave: "Well, this is not an easy decision ... I doubt if there is one answer for ... One could do a number of things ..."

With the beginning of 1945 came a fateful year. We knew that many parts of Poland had been liberated by the Russians, and that it was only a matter of time before the Germans would have to retreat from our part as well.

The Germans themselves were aware that their time was running out, and this very knowledge propelled them into increasingly vicious retaliation. More and more their behavior was like that of a wounded wild beast, which strikes out before it dies with all its fury and fading strength. We could not help but conclude that although time brought us closer to our liberation, it also brought us closer to disaster. We must not let the ever-present threats paralyze us; we must guard against them more vigilantly than ever. Each time my sister and I left the house, one or the other of my parents told us: "Concentrate on what is happening around. Be very careful. Avoid danger!"

As I walked through the streets of Kielce delivering my rolls or buying supplies, I noticed more Germans around. But they were not like the Nazis I had grown used to. Most of them were either very young, barely teenagers, or old men. They walked in groups, carrying their machine guns in a ready position. They, too, anticipated danger.

It was clear that the end was coming. Those Germans who could fight were sent to the front. Those who were left behind were either disabled or too old for battle. In my sister's club, few of the officers were under sixty and many were veterans with disabilities. When no one else was around these old, disabled officers confided that they had had enough. They wanted to go home and forget the whole thing.

Still the official press denied any losses and spoke about continuing victories. None of us took these reports seriously. We looked upon them as jokes, jokes that we desperately hoped would end soon.

Then one night we woke up to the noise of bombs falling, to be followed later by artillery fire. Air raid sirens sounded throughout the city. Like many compounds, ours had a common shelter. To reach it one had to cross the courtyard. Through our kitchen window we saw neighbors running for cover. But how could we join them? Officially my parents did not exist. They would have to stay in the apartment. Despite my father's urgings that we should go to the shelter, my sister and I refused to leave them.

At first bombs seemed to be falling all around us, but the explosions soon gave way to increased artillery exchanges. This meant that the Russians were nearby and we could expect them almost at any moment. When a lull came in the firing, Stefa and Basia rejoined us. Neighbors had been asking about my sister and me and perhaps our absence had puzzled them, even made some of them suspicious.

Intensive fire exchanges started again, so close that the walls were shaking. For a long time after that, none of us dared to leave the apartment—to go outside would be to risk getting killed in the crossfire. But the longer we huddled there, the more anxious and impatient we became. Though none of us said it, I think all of us must have felt how preposterous it would be to die here, now, almost at the end of our ordeal. Finally Stefa, who hardly ever made suggestions, insisted that we must all seek safety together, and my parents conceded that the time had come for even them to leave. We decided that at the next lull in the shooting, we would all try to reach the shelter, and that once we arrived there Stefa would explain that two of her cousins had arrived unexpectedly, in flight from the battle. We agreed that, even at the risk of being considered rude, the "cousins" would not talk to anyone.

Soon, dragging the baskets of food we had packed, we began to crawl toward the shelter. We were not quite halfway there when the firing started again. Although full dark had come we could see the bullets passing over our heads. "Keep moving, but stay close to the ground," my father ordered in a whisper. Again I lost all track of time, inching forward, almost flat on my stomach, glimpsing the others out of the corners of my eyes, too absorbed in what I was doing to pay much attention to the whine of bullets overhead, or even to feel scared.

We joined our neighbors almost unobserved. No one was interested in Stefa's explanation about her cousins. The shooting continued for what seemed like hours, but it had become increasingly sporadic and scattered—neither bombardment nor an artillery battle—although it was still close by. We were sure that the Germans would have to give up. The question was how soon.

Finally all was quiet. We waited in silence for a resumption of fire, but it did not come. Light began to penetrate the hole that was the entrance to our cellar, so we knew that day had come. Still we sat there waiting, in total silence, not speaking, not communicating with one another in any way at all. Perhaps we were all stunned by the enormity of the event.

Then, in the distance, we heard male voices. Could it be? I strained my ears. This time I was sure. They spoke Russian! Now our own small group did exchange glances. There was no need for words: we had decided to leave.

We came out into a free world. All was silent. There was no wild excitement. There was nothing, and I felt nothing except exhaustion. We looked at one another in disbelief. Was this the end?

When we entered our apartment, I was surprised that it looked just the same as when we had left. Had I expected some miraculous transformation? But a miracle of sorts had taken place, and we began to hug one another as we kept repeating that it was over, that we were alive, that we were free. But the reality of the event did not register for a long time. The change was too sudden for us to grasp it fully.

Through the windows we saw the first Russian soldiers. They moved cautiously, searching for hiding Germans. In a little while, some Poles came out from their houses and proceeded to greet the Russians enthusiastically. We stayed indoors and continued to watch, amazed that they should dare to venture out into the streets not yet free of danger. We continued to hear sporadic gunfire, but did not know whether a few Germans were still offering resistance or the Russians were simply shooting those they found.

Midday came, and the Russians continued to comb the area for Nazis. Then, from the house of a young woman across the street, who had been friendly with the Nazis, we saw a German officer come out with his hands in the air. If it had not been for those raised hands and his uniform, I would never have guessed that he was a German. His shoulders were stooped, his head was as low as his position would allow it to be, and he walked cautiously, as if shaking with fear. Until then all the Nazis walked stiffly erect, with a sure gait and an arrogant expression on their faces, as if the whole world belonged to them and the rest of us were lowly creatures not fit to live. But this first Nazi I saw surrender looked like a broken man, devoid of all energy and spirit, an image of total submission.

Before long we knew that the transformation we had just witnessed was not peculiar to one man alone. All the other Germans who were giving themselves up looked humble, frightened, and demoralized, and we grew accustomed to that look. But it was surprising how many Germans emerged from our neighborhood. As the Russians kept rounding them up, they seemed to multiply.

Those Poles who were on the streets obviously derived a vast enjoyment from the whole process, jeering, cursing, and spitting at newly captured Nazis, cheering on the Russians as they shoved and hit their prisoners. We continued to watch through our windows, still in a sort of trance, and the drama unfolding before us seemed no more real than if it had in fact been a drama played out in a theater.

Later that afternoon there came a knock at the door, and this time my parents felt no need to hide. A few Russians, all friendly looking, came in, and we noticed that one of them, an officer, appeared Jewish. He looked around, apparently searching for something, and then hesitantly said in Polish, "My parents, they used to live here, where are they?" We understood then that he was one of those Polish Jews who had left for the Russian Zone, and that for whatever reasons he had been unable to send back for his parents.

Who could give him an answer? With a gentle disbelief, my father asked, "Don't you know what happened to Jews?" The officer must have known, but he had failed to consider that it might apply to his parents. He nodded in distress, accepting the knowledge, and yet kept repeating as if to himself, "Where are my parents? Where are they?" No one could help him. Nothing more was said, and he turned to the door and left, followed in silence by the whole group.

Not only the remaining Germans but their collaborators as well were subject to prosecution. Included
among them were all the young women who had
associated with the Nazis, and who almost overnight
had found themselves without protection of any sort.
Their Polish friends made themselves invisible, and
the Polish patriots helped the Russians round them
up. Teresa and the young woman who lived across
from us were among them. After they were arrested,
their heads were shaved and they were paraded down
the middle of the street throughout the city, facing
large and hostile crowds who had come out specifically to humiliate them. As they marched along, these
girls were bombarded with jeers and vituperation;
rotten apples were thrown at them, even stones, and
not even the Russians dared to interfere.

In this period immediately following the German
surrender, neither the pathetic look of these girls
nor their mortification helped to mollify the people.
On the contrary, the more exhausted and wretched
these women appeared, the nastier and more men-
acing the mood of the crowd became. It was hard to
believe that only a very short while before at least
some of those who now indulged in an orgy of jeers
and threats had been indifferent to those girls or
had even approved of them. The speed with which
the public mood could reverse itself astonished me.

Everything, indeed, was changing too drastically
and too fast. Even our relationship with the Homars
had changed. They behaved toward us in a con-
strained, uneasy kind of way that made us feel uncomfortable and somewhat at a loss. Was it hard for
them to accept us as free people, who were no longer
dependent on them? We continued to regard them
as our benefactors, acutely conscious that it was only
thanks to them that we were alive.

At least a partial explanation soon emerged. One
evening all of us, including Ziutka and Tadek, gathered around the table for tea and bread. The Homars

were more tense than ever, and all of us were uncomfortable. For a while we engaged in small talk,
although we all felt that eventually something else
would have to be said. Finally Ziutka, the bluntest of
them all, started out hesitantly: "Well . . ." Stammer-
ing and embarrassed, she continued, "We want to
ask you . . ." And then, without looking at anyone,
she finally came out with it. The Homars wanted us
to leave Kielce as Poles, without revealing our true
identity. They did not want anyone to know that
they had helped a Jewish family to survive.

When Ziutka finished, we were stunned. There
was a long silence. Not I, not my sister, not my
mother could think of anything to say. In the end,
my father, in an even but sadly quiet voice, agreed.
He added that we were extremely grateful for what
they had done for us, and that they ought to be
proud of having saved our lives. His tone was flat, as
if at last he was tired. The Homars' request may
have been too much even for a strong man like him.
We avoided looking at him and at one another.

Without commenting on what my father had said,
Ziutka asked when we intended to leave. Clearly they
wanted us to do so as soon as possible.

Perhaps they were not actually sorry or ashamed
about having saved us, but they undoubtedly felt
that their friends and neighbors would not approve
of what they had done. We had no reason to doubt
that they were right. After all, they had to continue
living among these people, and they had to be concerned about their own safety. All this was logical
and reasonable enough. Why, then, were we so upset?

We were upset because they themselves failed to
reassure us that they were glad we were alive and
felt gratified by the part they played in our rescue.
Expressions of such sentiments would have dispelled
our doubts and lifted our spirits. Their failure to do
so left us hurt, bewildered, and with lingering
suspicions.

All of us welcomed the temporary relief that came with the ending of this awkward evening.

For years we had devoted all our energies to staying alive. For us, the future had meant being alive, and beyond that we had no plans. Now that the future was upon us we had no energy left to plan. Even my father did not talk about the future.

We did, however, take a first step, and tried to arrange for a return to Lublin. This was not easy. Trains were not running, so the only way one could travel was by car, and except for military vehicles there were hardly any cars on the road. With the arrival of the Russians, the money we had left had lost its value. Fortunately we still had some jewelry and gold, and part of that could be used to pay for our trip. Eager to see us go, Tadek and Ziutka joined in the effort to find us transportation. After a considerable search we located a military truck that was going to Lublin, with a driver who was willing to take us.

As we were actually parting from the Homars we were all moved. Except for my father and Tadek we all cried bittersweet tears. Hugging Waldek, I felt a tremendously deep sadness that dissolved all the misunderstandings and tensions. After all, we had gone through a great deal together. A wave of genuine love and affection swept us into one embrace after another, and into an exchange of fervent promises to be in close touch for ever and ever. How complicated it all was! So many conflicting emotions and thoughts were fighting one another that I could not even begin to understand the conflict taking place inside me.

We left in accordance with the Homars' request, as Polish relatives, but at that point no one was inquisitive about us. The trip in the back of the truck, over primitive, bumpy roads, was long and arduous. We continued to feel overwhelmed by the events of the last few days, and I was aware of a strange, acute disappointment because paradoxically I did not feel deliriously happy. The trip passed almost in total silence.

We reached Lublin at dusk. My father gave the driver our old address: Pijarska Number One. Why did he do that? Was it a sentimental move? That would have been out of character for my father. Did he expect the apartment to be waiting for us? We did not own the place, and we had left it many years before.

The truck came to a stop, and we all jumped down. Before us stood a ruin. Bombs must have demolished the entire street. We said nothing at all. I turned to my father, looking for strength, but for the first time he had no strength to give. He stood absorbed in his thoughts. He looked tired, so very tired. I wanted to reach out to him, to touch him and comfort him. I made no move. None of us made a sound. Still in silence, we climbed back into the truck, which once again started to move, this time toward our chemical factory.

Pressed into the corner of the truck, I was overcome by sadness. Around me was the city of Lublin. My city. I could hear it. I could smell it. But neither its noises nor its smells were familiar. I felt like a stranger. Was this really the city I knew? I refused to look, afraid that what I saw might confirm my doubts. I closed my eyes instead.

Epilogue

———◆◆———

Around me was the city of Lublin. My city. I could hear it. I could smell it. But neither its noises nor its smells were familiar. I felt like a stranger. Was this really the city I knew? I refused to look, afraid that what I saw might confirm my doubts. I closed my eyes instead.

THUS did the original edition of *Dry Tears* end. Why, I have often been asked, did I choose this point to end my story? My answers were evasive—usually, I replied that I was saving the rest for another book. The truth is that I ended the story where I did because at that time I could go no further.

With liberation, my struggle for survival ended only to be replaced by other less concrete, less tangible kinds of struggle that had to do with personal losses, Jewish identity, and the seeming indifference of others to our survival. To delve into these complex issues would have required a new and prolonged effort, one that emotionally I am not yet prepared to undertake.

When Oxford University Press decided to republish *Dry Tears* in a paperback edition my editor, Susan Rabiner, tried to convince me that a bridging between my past and present would remove that up-in-the-air feeling of the original ending. Even though I agreed intellectually with Susan's arguments, I was not yet ready for them emotionally.

What follows is a compromise between a new intellectual willingness to recall what happened after liberation and a continued emotional reluctance to face it.

* * *

On that first evening, we stood at the gate of our chemical factory with our meager belongings. I knew that at the entrance to the right were the janitor's living quarters. We waited for my father's move. He hesitated. Then with a determined, sudden gesture he knocked at the door. A voice extended an invitation to come in. In a moment we were facing the old janitor Jan and his wife Genia. Their expression of surprise was followed by an uneasy smile: "You are alive? Come in, come . . . it looks like you just came back! . . . Welcome, welcome . . . make yourself comfortable, you will feel comfortable here." Both reached to relieve us of our luggage. Both seemed eager to make us feel at home, while they continued to tell us how glad they were to see us. They made us wash up and rest.

The place was warm and cozy. Our hosts were friendly. They kept assuring us that we would be comfortable; by assuming that we would stay they made us feel particularly welcome as they tried to anticipate and answer both the spoken and unspoken questions.

Yes, there were many Jews in Lublin. They came back from all over. The Jews were very rich. And the Russians were giving them all kinds of privileges. They had it good. There is a special center where all the Jews went to find relatives. Yes, they knew where it was. On Rybna Street. The address conjured up a vision of delapidated ugliness.

We were in a warm, large kitchen. A massive table dominated the room with surrounding chairs, some of which were now in disarray. At our hosts' insistence we sat at the table while they busied themselves with preparations of a meal.

When I began to look around it dawned on me that I was seeing familiar objects. The table was covered with our table cloth, the silver was ours. I continued to recognize more and more items. With recognition came a strong feeling of discomfort and an urge to run away.

My father confronted me with one of his steel-like looks, and as he did his gray-blue eyes ordered me to silence. His seemingly expressionless face told me that he noticed just as I did, but all this was of no consequence. My mother tried to look and act pleasantly, too pleasantly. I could not help thinking Why is she so happy? Was this her way of covering up what she must have felt? My sister looked ill at ease. We tried to exchange a fleeting smile that died under father's piercing eyes even before it had a chance to appear.

My attention moved to Jan and Genia, both of whom seemed unaware of the tension; they continued to treat us in a relaxed and warm way. No doubt they had gotten hold of our possessions before the Nazis could get to them. Perhaps they had forgotten, or never knew, that these things were once an intimate part of our lives?

Good naturedly, Jan and Genia took turns urging us to eat. I was too preoccupied to notice what I was swallowing. I also tried to hear what Jan was saying. Then I began to wonder. If so many Jews survived how come none of those whom my father inquired about are here?

What about the German commissioner whom the Nazis installed as head of our factory and who had been kind to us, arranging to shelter us in the beginning and holding our gold and jewelry until we sent for it? He ran away as soon as Lublin was liberated: "He is hiding, don't worry the Russians will find him!" Why did he think we wanted the Russians to get him? Then Genia added that they knew where his daughter Danuta lived; the authorities had nothing against Danuta. My father, sounding matter of fact, asked for her address, and registered the answer.

The government now owned our factory. The new director was disliked by the workers—he did not know how to run the place.

Then Jan told us that the building in the garden, in the back of the factory, had an empty apartment. He felt that we ought to apply at the police station for permission to move in. He followed this suggestion with an assurance that we were welcome to stay with them. I was glad to hear him say it, even though I would have preferred to be somewhere else. Was it because too many things reminded me of my past, a past I could not face, not then and not later? In fact, not for over thirty years.

When the evening came to an end the janitor and his wife moved the table against the wall to make room for mattresses. Clean linen, pillows, and comforters transformed these mattresses into comfortable beds.

As I stretched out next to my sister, I became aware of the familiarity of the comforters and linens. I was tired but sleep refused to come. By the breathing sounds, I knew that the rest of my family was awake. Yet, we did not communicate. Were we reluctant to disturb our hosts or was there too much to say?

As I lay there with eyes wide open, covered by our old covers, many competing sensations clamored for attention. When they came together with glimpses from the past I pushed them away. I refused to deal with my past. I wished I were somewhere else. My old self had belonged here but not I.

So many of our belongings switched masters, becoming a part of someone else's lives; objects have no loyalty. It was as if my finding them so well adjusted to the new owners mocked my claim to them. Their settled presence made me an intruder.

I shuddered at the thought that all this would have been the same even if I were no more. Many of us fantasize about our own death. Is this how I would have felt had I attended my own funeral?

Early in the morning, eager to find surviving relatives and friends, we took leave of our friendly hosts. As we reached the street my father urged us not to think about the possessions we had recognized. He explained that Jan had appropriated what might have otherwise gone to waste; it was better to see him enjoy these objects than strangers or Nazis. Besides, my father insisted that it was not worth bothering about and advised us never to mention that these objects belonged to us, especially not to our hosts.

To reach the Jewish center we had to pass the length of Lubartowska Street, the main artery of the commercial part of the city. Our candle factory was located at the edge of the street. To prevent the Nazis from confiscating this factory my father had transferred it to one of his employees, Mr. Pys, with the understanding that after the war it would be returned. On that morning as we approached the factory gate ready to go inside, we hesitated. My father's voice would not let us go in: "This is not the time; we must go to the center first!"

Without stopping, we reached the neglected, uninviting, old part of the city. The Jewish center was located in a rundown building, on one of those dark and narrow streets that admitted little light and where the protruding cobblestones had no chance to dry from the rain or dirty water poured over them by its inhabitants. Noises signifying the presence of many people greeted us at the dimly lit stairways. With each step the noise became louder and with it came a strong odor of cheap tobacco and sweat.

The center consisted of three connecting small rooms, each furnished with a desk, a chair, and a file cabinet. Green, poorly painted, and peeling walls were covered with differently shaped papers that had messages, names, and addresses scribbled all over them. This was one more way of finding relatives and friends; one more effort, in addition to the official registration.

Poorly lit and poorly ventilated, the place was filled with people, talking and gesticulating in Polish, Yiddish, Hungarian, and languages I could not recognize.

They appeared anxious and worried, as each separately tried to catch the attention of the persons sitting behind the desks, who in turn, must have had a hard time deciding whom to listen to.

It was obvious that, as a group, we could not reach these officials. My father suggested that the rest of us move closer to the wall, while he alone tried to make the necessary inquiries.

Away from the thickest crowd I found a wall to lean against. I began to contemplate these strangers; it seemed that none of them cared about us nor about any of the others. Each person was there alone, each seemed oblivious to the presence of others. Their attention was focused on the officials behind the desks. What did I have in common with this mass of people? Did I belong here? I felt slightly dizzy and nauseous. Next to me my mother and sister looked as uncomfortably tense. No doubt they too would have preferred to be somewhere else. Where?

After what seemed like a long, long time I was relieved to see my father make his way toward us. I looked at him closely, trying to guess what news he brought. Around his mouth was a suggestion, a touch, of a bemused smile. Yet his eyes expressed no joy: "Well, we have one relative and there are a few people we used to know." It turned out that this relative, Mietek, was my father's brother's brother-in-law. I did not remember him at all. Maybe I never met him. The news, however, conjured up an image of my Aunt Sylvia, my Uncle Gershon's wife, an unattractive woman who was perpetually depressed. Sylvia and her son had been shot by the Nazis. Gershon left for Russia. How odd that Sylvia's brother was the only relative we had!

In the street, away from the noise I realized that my mother was crying. Father tried to console her: "It is still early, they may come back. Why cry until you know for sure?" Did he believe it himself? His voice did not sound convincing.

I began to wonder whom my mother had expected to find. During the war we had learned of the murder of most of her relatives. She had never discussed her hopes with us. Now, too, she said nothing. Only her crying spoke of her newly shattered, never realistic, dreams. She continued to weep in a quiet, resigned way, a way that expressed more pain than any loud display ever could have.

Then my father shared with us a few facts. A little over one hundred Jews came back to Lublin. Some of them were not even from the city proper, but from adjacent towns. Among them were only two intact families. Now we became the third.

Before the war Lublin had a Jewish population of forty thousand. Only a little over one hundred were left! Bewildered, I wondered how Jan and Genia could have said that many Jews had come back? As if in answer to my silent question I heard my father say: "Some may still come, as we did." Few did. In the end, the estimated figure for Jewish survivors in Lublin did not exceed one hundred and fifty.

Mietek, our relative, lived close to the chemical factory in the commercial section of Lublin. Later we learned that most returning Jews settled in this part of town. Now, more so than ever before, Jews tried to stay close to each other. Not only did they live near each other, but they also felt close to each other.

Perhaps this handful of survivors tried each to be family to the others, to act as a partial substitute for all those who failed to return?

Mietek's building was in a much better condition than the one we had just left. As we neared his apartment we could hear Yiddish being spoken. Then an opened door revealed a spacious room with a large corner stove identifying it as a kitchen. It was an inviting place flooded with the bright morning sun. A group of adults sat around a large table. The scattered dishes, glasses, silver, and the variety of foods told of an unfinished breakfast. An attractive young woman caught my eye first, and right next to her was an older woman. The rest were four men. Which of them was our relative? I experienced no flicker of recognition, no hint. Then, suddenly a man of medium height jumped up as if prodded by some powerful force. He had an egg-shaped, slightly overgrown, partly bald head. A friendly smile revealed two rows of white teeth, clearly the most attractive feature he had. His black eyes, although small, were expressive in a lively sort of way. Without waiting for positive confirmation, he threw himself first at my father's neck and then at my mother's. In a moment all three were exchanging hugs and embraces. Mietek kept repeating "How good that you are here, how wonderful to see you!" Soon my sister and I were subjected to the same enthusiastic greeting. Thus, we met our only surviving relative. With a proud and warm smile he turned to the others: "My relatives. I have relatives! Imagine!" His mood was contagious. All, including those we had just met, were happy to be a part of the reunion.

My immediate reactions to this new relative were positive. Time only helped to reconfirm these first impressions. Mietek was outgoing and generous.

As we were being introduced to the others, it was inevitable that some questions and answers had to be exchanged. What kind of information did we share?

The young woman was Mietek's fiancée. She and one of the men, her brother, survived, as they put it, on the Aryan side, among Christians. The older woman, her sister, had been a concentration camp inmate. Mietek and the two other men had fought together in a Polish partisan group. We, in turn, told them that we too had survived on the Aryan side. Beyond such statements that only identified generally the ways in which each of us survived, little else was said. None of us was able to speak specifically of our own wartime experiences. None of us asked for elaborations or details from the others. Later I realized that if, as it rarely happened, one of us felt like saying more, more than just identifying the mode of survival, such information had to be volunteered by the speaker. It was never requested by the listener. Somehow, automatically, without discussion, we learned not to probe into each other's wartime past. Even today, when it comes to my close friends, I know few details of their war experiences. This does not mean that we refrain from talking about things that matter, or that we don't care about each other. All it means is that stirring up memories of what happened during the war can hurt too much, and we must each choose our own time to endure this necessary pain.

During this first encounter with our relative, our conversation moved quickly into the then-present. Naturally and without boasting, Mietek told us that he was financially well off. He was involved in an export-import business that was making him rich. He had money to spare and wanted to lend us as much as we like and for as long as we wanted it. My father accepted his offer. From then on, for quite a while, we lived on borrowed funds. Our newly found relative was not only generous with money. He insisted on being helpful in any way he could, and this included time and valuable advice.

Indeed, Mietek's connection at the police helped

us get a permit for the vacant apartment on the factory grounds. That same afternoon, with Mietek's and Jan's help, we were installed in a two-room home.

One of the rooms was a large kitchen that was to serve as a living room, dining room, and bedroom for my sister and me. The second, smaller room was converted into my parent's bedroom. The furniture was sparse. We had one kitchen table surrounded by benches, mattresses instead of beds, and one little closet. Mietek and his friends supplied us with utensils, dishes, linen, covers, and pillowcases. Still, this was a great improvement over the overcrowded apartment we had in Kielce. And neither the meager furniture nor the bare floors and windows prevented us from feeling good about this place. After years of no privacy we were delighted to have a home of our own.

Mietek and his friends insisted that we spend the first evening in their place. They wanted us to meet other Jews who had reached the city before we did. Of those who came only one was a girl my age: Ania. I had met her before, and knew who she was but we had never been friends. Among the other guests my parents and my sister recognized only a few acquaintances. Yet all those present, whether they knew us or not, made a fuss over us. They all tried to be helpful, offering assistance and advice.

Right after the liberation, Jews were supportive of each other. Those who came earlier and had apartments felt an obligation to offer food and lodgings to the new arrivals and to those who were only passing through our city. Being friends or knowing the people was not a precondition for offers of help; the practice applied to total strangers. In fact, among those who stopped in Lublin were Hungarian Jews returning to their homes from concentration camps. They too benefited from Jewish hospitality. Soon we followed this practice and had a stream of survivors pass through our modest apartment.

My parents never lost their enthusiasm for education. Practically the first week, with borrowed money, they hired several tutors who were to give us private instruction. The idea was to catch up on our lost years of schooling. Four years older than I, my sister began to study for the high school diploma (*matura*). Not yet fourteen, it was assumed that after a few months I would pass a special examination and would become a second year high school student. In typical old world style, neither my sister's nor my wishes were considered when it came to educational decisions. We were simply told that we would have to devote all our energy to study. And indeed it did not even occur to us that there might have been an alternative.

In 1945 the Russians, Poles, and Jews were each caught in their own special webs of traditions, ideologies, and perceptions. Often incompatible, these different ideas and values could and did lead to dangerous conflicts.

Months before the official end of the war Poland was under Soviet control, a fact that most Poles experienced as a national humiliation; a war had been fought, an occupation endured, and an underground war waged, simply to substitute a Russian occupation for the German one.

Russian-Polish hostility had a long history, reaching back to the beginnings of each as a nation. In the more recent past, for over one hundred years, a large part of Poland was ruled by a succession of oppressive Russian Czars. Only with the end of World War I, when Poland reemerged as an independent nation, did it reclaim these occupied territories. But the physical disappearance of the Russians did not reduce the Pole's resentment and distrust. Instead, they were convinced that the Soviets were eager to prove themselves by reestablishing the Russian Empire at least to the old Czarist borders. Everything Russian was highly suspect; as a consequence few

Poles found communism appealing. When the Polish government outlawed the Communist Party in 1938 it had a membership of twenty thousand. Following the introduction of this law some Polish Communists were imprisoned, some escaped to the Soviet Union, still others went into hiding.

In 1939, after Germany's takeover, the Poles formed a government in exile, in London. Included in this new government were representatives of four major political blocks: the Socialists, the Peasants, the Social Democrats, and the large segment of Nationalists and Catholics. Each of these blocks was in turn subdivided into subgroups, with each reflecting a wide range of ideological shadings. Traditional Polish individualism and the closely related diversity of values defies an overall explanation of Poland's political life. In fact, from the beginning, the Polish government in London, precisely because it was made up of so many competing, and even hostile political entities, had a hard time formulating clear cut policies. At best this government achieved a loosely connected broad kind of unity.

One arm of the official armed forces of the government in exile was the illegal underground in Nazi-occupied Poland, known as the Home Army (A.K.). The Home Army, just as its political counterpart in London, was a conglomeration of many groups, also reflecting a wide range of political ideologies, each taking its clues crom a different political segment in London. The entire A.K. was made up of semiautonomous units that often disagreed with each others' policies. At times, even when faced with a common enemy, these illegal underground groups acted out their mutual hostilities.

Excluded both from the Polish government in exile and from the Home Army in Poland were two small political entities: on the extreme right were the Fascists and on the extreme left the Communists. The Fascists established their own underground, also composed of loosely connected splinter groups, known as the National Armed Forces (NSZ or Falanga). Some of these Fascist groups were fighting the Germans, the Jews, the Communists, and factions of the Home Army (A.K.).

Because of the Russian-German alliance that began on September 17, 1939, the handful of Polish Communists had to remain inactive until June 1941, when Hitler invaded Russia. Only after the German attack on Russia did they start organizing into an anti-Nazi unit. At that time a small Polish Communist Party emerged (PPR) and their underground fighters were known as the Peoples Army (GL). Russian partisans became the natural partners for these Polish Communists. The Soviets, thinking about their future domination of Poland even then, began to exaggerate the sheer number and fighting power of Polish Communists—a practice they never abandoned.

When in 1945 the Russians took over Poland they knew that the overwhelming majority of Poles, including the loosely integrated underground, were loyal to the Polish government in exile. The Russians also knew that support for this Polish government in London was coupled with resentment about Soviet presence in Poland. This awareness, however, in no way implied a willingness to accommodate. On the contrary, the Soviets were determined to consolidate their grip over the newly acquired territories. As a first step they set up a government filled with Polish Communists and others whose loyalty to Russia was well tested. Communist controlled, this Polish government undermined and eventually destroyed the legitimacy of the Polish government in exile. The American government, eager to avoid a break with its wartime ally, protested, but only mildly. This acquiescent passivity of the Americans helped speed up the end of the London group as the official government of Poland. The Poles had a right to feel betrayed.

But some Poles were less willing to yield to Russian

threats than the Americans and the postwar British. Parts of the Home Army challenged the Soviet presence by refusing to disband. Through acts of sabotage they set out to undermine the Communist influence in Poland.

Adding to the already existent chaos were clandestine activities of various underground groups not associated with the Home Army. These were the splinter groups of the far right, the Fascists (NSZ).

Faced with a deteriorating situation the Russians did not give up. Instead, they launched a ruthless persecution of all unauthorized underground groups. Their special aim was to destroy the powerful forces of the A.K. Many people were arrested only because they had been associated with the Home Army during its anti-Nazi days. Many of those arrested had nothing to do with postwar illegal operations. Because all former A.K. members were in danger, some tried to conceal their wartime affiliations. A virtual witch hunt ensued. But more than a total disregard for human rights was needed. To subjugate these unruly forces required both a single-minded passion and time. Indeed order was restored only in 1947.

How did the Jews fit into this Polish-Russian confrontation? Unlike the Poles, Jews defined the Soviets as liberators, welcoming them warmly. In turn, at least initially, the Russians also treated the surviving Jews with special consideration.

To consolidate their power the Soviets needed the support of the local population. They knew that for this support they could rely and trust the Jews more than the Poles. Moreover, among Jews who returned from Russia some were seasoned Communists. This last group in particular could be relied on. As a result, many of them were offered high political and police positions.

Not surprisingly, this close Jewish-Russian cooperation did not pass unnoticed. When some high Jewish officials became involved in the persecution of the Polish underground, all Jews were blamed for it. Such persecutions were seen as proof that the Jews were in fact the enemies of the Polish people. No doubt the traditionally strong Polish anti-Semitism had acted as a fertile ground for the development and acceptance of these anti-Jewish perceptions. Added to this well-established anti-Semitism must have been Polish resentment created by Jewish efforts to reclaim their property. These were properties taken over by the local population after being abandoned by fleeing or forcibly removed Jewish owners.

When, for example, my father went to see Mr. Pys, the Pole who ran our candle factory, he was greeted with open hostility. And it mattered little that, remembering the help formerly offered us by this Pole, my father had broached the subject of the factory gently and tactfully. Mr. Pys lost his temper and began to shout: "What do you think, you Jews? You can come from nowhere and retake what rightfully belongs to us?"

After that we had to rely on legal channels. Without much difficulty the factory was returned to us and when the place officially changed hands Mr. Pys's parting words were, "This is not the end, you will be sorry for that!"

Soon alarming news began to reach us. Jews were being murdered. Small rural places became particularly unsafe. There the extreme rightist faction of the Polish underground seemed to operate with impunity. In this chaotic situation however, it was hard to establish responsibility for specific Jewish deaths. It is estimated that in Poland, in the postwar period, fifteen hundred Jews were murdered by Poles.

The Russians tried to protect Jewish lives. They also treated the Jews leniently by returning large enterprises to them. This, as it turned out, was only a temporary measure. Later on most private establishments were reclaimed by the state. But in the con-

fusion of postwar Poland this was still in the unknown future. In the meantime, we were among
those who benefited from the generous policy. In
addition to the candle factory, my father received half
of the chemical factory with the provision that he
become the director for the entire enterprise.

As the new director my father was determined to
improve his employees' lot. He had the workers'
kitchen modernized and installed a new cook and a
dietician. Next he ordered the redecoration of the
recreational hall, refurbished the library, and added
special rooms for music listening. His workers were
impressed and felt that such dramatic changes ought
to be commemorated with a special ceremony.

A workers' committee organized an evening. They
issued invitations to the press and government officials. As part of these festivities they planned
speeches that were to pay tribute to my father's efforts. Eventually the ceremony turned into a political
rally filled with propaganda slogans, with my father
being referred to as a proletarian fighter, a revolu-
tionary, and a devoted Communist. The speakers
seemed carried away by their own exaggerated ut-
terances and the crowd greeted each of them with
emotional and wild applause.

This was definitely more than my father had bar-
gained for. My father felt uncomfortable when people made a fuss over him, especially in public. That
evening, as I watched his exterior calmness, I knew
that he was cringing on the inside. At home, when
alone with us, he dismissed it all as "too much unnecessary fuss." Besides, he was apolitical, an indi-
vidualist who wouldn't adhere to any particular party
line, especially one so constraining as that of the
Communists. He had always treated his workers with
respect and consideration. This treatment, however,
was unrelated to a political ideology but rather to a
combination of humanitarianism and good business
sense. Indeed, while he cared about his workers, he

rarely spoke about his feelings, preferring to express them in deeds. Most of my father's workers knew and those who did not soon realized that his efforts on their behalf were motivated by a genuine concern about their welfare.

I lived in a shielded environment, the daughter of a man whom many admired. I was aware of my privileged position and liked it. At that time I tried to please my parents by channeling all my efforts into school work. Though intensive study left me little room for social contacts, even in my protective isolation disturbing news about anti-Semitism that had led to attacks against Jews kept reaching me.

Ever since I first heard Jan mention the commissioner I knew that my father would try to help him. During the war this German had treated us decently and we knew of no atrocities or crimes that he had committed against others. It would have been out of my father's character if he had not tried to repay for the man's past kindness.

Soon my father met with the commissioner's daughter Danuta. He gave her money and offered other help. In fact, he was convinced that he could rehabilitate the man by testifying on his behalf. But Danuta remained unconvinced. She refused to divulge her parents' hiding place, and insisted that she did not know where they were. She continued to accept our money, but would not take any advice and never budged from her initial position. To my father's disappointment, even this financial help could not continue. One day Danuta disappeared without a trace.

My parents must have been in touch with the Homars because one day they told us that Basia and Stefa were coming and that Basia became engaged to one of the neighborhood young men, Rysiek. I remembered Rysiek as a tall, awkward youth, kind and quiet. Both had worked in the same factory and the romance might have started after we had left

Kielce because I never knew that he and Basia were sweethearts. Convinced as I was that to marry one had to be madly in love, I was happy for Basia.

When my parents were told about the engagement they offered to supply the bridal trousseau. For this reason, Stefa and her daughter were coming to stay with us, while a seamstress hired by my parents was to sew the bride's wardrobe and whatever else she might need in her new home.

At that point we had moved into a spacious and well-furnished apartment. Before our guests' arrival one of the rooms was converted into a combination bedroom and sewing room, with half of the area filled with sewing equipment and materials.

I was both eager and apprehensive about this visit. With their arrival would come a reminder of a world so very far away—a world that occasionally took on a distant dreamlike quality, one that I preferred not to be reminded about.

When I actually faced Basia and Stefa again a warm feeling of affection swept over me. I wanted to see them happy and relaxed. The rest of my family must have felt the same way because each tried to be attentive and solicitous.

But Stefa and Basia seemed ill at ease, not relaxed at all. It was natural for us to inquire about all those who were left in Kielce. The information we received attested only to their well-being but not much else. After that brief exchange we were searching for topics for discussion.

I was glad that for each of us next day and the days that followed were filled with intensive activities. I was particularly grateful that I had to go to school and then devote a lot of time to homework. My mother took care of entertaining Basia and Stefa. At first the three were busy shopping for additional materials; then Basia had to try on the unfinished clothes. In what was left of their time the Homars tried to make themselves useful by assisting the seamstress in different tasks. I realized how involved the making of a bride's trousseau could be. I also realized that for us the many intricate decisions that had to be made in connection with all the sewing were a blessing in disguise. During our shared meals they provided us with vital topics for discussion.

Between our visitors and us there was something unspoken—something that impeded a free, relaxed communication. Perhaps it had to do with the way we parted. Perhaps it had to do with our reversed positions of dependence and independence. Whatever it was, it created a strain that refused to go away. We had little to say to each other and none of us felt good about it.

Stefa and Basia stayed for two weeks. And when the time came to accompany them to the train station they each had a hard time carrying their newly acquired possessions, a sign of my parent's generosity. We parted with hugs and embraces and wishes for a good and happy future. All of us behaved properly, said the right things—and yet something was missing. As I watched them depart I was filled with a strange mixture of regret, guilt, and relief. What was it? Were our worlds so far apart? So impossible to bridge? We were not invited to the wedding, and we never saw the Homars again.

The end of the fall brought with it unusually balmy weather. Late one afternoon I watched the sun linger on, as if reluctant to take leave. At the factory production had stopped a while ago. I welcomed the freshly arrived silence that followed the cacophony of over two hundred employees all rushing out of the factory and homeward within minutes of each other.

With most of my homework done I looked at the kitchen clock, wondering where my father was. My mother was busy near the stove, and my sister, oblivious to the world, was engrossed in a book. What a shame to be cooped up inside an apartment on a day

like this! I sat on the doorsteps listening to the stillness, watching the plants, the trees, all telling about
the approaching new season. Once more I thought
that my father was unusually late. I liked waiting for
him. I would meet him with a hug, a smile, and few
words. We understood each others' silences.

Then I noticed my father coming in my direction.
He walked differently. Something about him had
changed. Something about him reminded me of the
tiredness he showed shortly after we were liberated.
When he greeted me with an absentminded, automatic smile I knew that something terrible must have
happened. Quietly I followed him into the house.
After only a tentative greeting gesture, I heard him
say: "I have serious news that we must keep secret."
We were used to secrets. But what we heard that
afternoon left us bewildered and at a loss.

My father had had a visitor, a brother of one of
his workers. The man was a double agent. He worked
for the secret police and was also a member of the
illegal Polish underground. As a member of the underground he had learned that his organization was
planning to assassinate my father. Aware that in the
middle of the day he visits his candle factory, they
had worked out a plan to shoot him there. All was
set with a specific plan and date. There were just
three days left. Three men were to take part in the
operation. First, one of them would ask to see my
father, ostensibly to conduct some business. Once this
man was safe in my father's office, two others would
come in and cover the rest of the employees. They
would cut the phones, while the first one would shoot
my father. Then, all three would move outside and
into a waiting car. It was all very simple.

What did this double agent propose? The police
were interested in catching the men in action. They
would like to do the following: They would plant
agents in and around the factory, particularly behind the doors of my father's office. As soon as the

prospective killer entered, he would be overpowered by two secret policemen. They expected to catch all participants, including those in the getaway car. On the designated day everyone, including my father, would have to behave naturally and follow the usual routine. Without my father's cooperation, however, the secret police could not proceed with these plans. As for the rest of the factory employees, they could be told only at the last moment.

What had my father decided? He had agreed to the man's proposition. This upset my mother: "If there is shooting, and there will be, they may kill you!" Of course, she was right, but my father's answer was: "This is a chance to fight back. I had to agree."

The decision was made. I felt oppressed and scared. My world, the new and comfortable world, was once more falling apart. We had three days left. During that time we were expected to act as if nothing special was about to happen. My father made us promise not to mention anything to anyone. Even among ourselves we were not to refer to the matter again. Following these instructions we did not communicate with words. Our eyes and the long heavy silences confirmed that we shared the same fears.

On the day my father dressed with his customary care. I asked permission to stay home.

On the way out my father managed to produce one of those detached smiles. He whispered: "All will be well, don't worry!" He left abruptly. We moved to a window and watched him cross the courtyard with his decisive habitual gait. Then a factory door swallowed him up, preventing us from following him further.

And what if I will never see him again? Gloomy thoughts and strange emotions were taking hold of me. None of it seemed to make sense. It was as if someone else was talking inside me. Who? Saying what?

It would take hours before we would know. What were we to do with all that useless time?

My mother knew: "We must clean the apartment and do a thorough job!" Never before was our place attacked with such vigor and determination. But even our energetic activity did not prevent time from stretching into eternity. Twelve o'clock came and passed. After that I could not take my eyes off the clock. I continued to clean yet another object, mechanically like a robot.

Then the door opened suddenly and through it burst in the young receptionist from the candle factory. She was obviously out of breath as she shouted: "We are fine. Mr. Bawnik is fine. He will be here in a minute." We began to jump with joy and took turns hugging. Soon we were joined by my father; a satisfied but subdued man.

What had happened? The underground men had put up a fight. Two of them were killed, another ran away. One of the police agents was wounded. The car was caught, but only after the driver was wounded. None of the employees was hurt. As soon as the shooting started, all of them were flat on the floor. The police saw this operation as a victory. I doubt if my father shared their views. He became unusually pensive and refused to discuss or elaborate further.

The police insisted on placing guards around my father's office, while others patrolled the factory premises at all hours. We all tried to resume our usual activities. Then a typed, anonymous note reached the director's office. All it said was: "We know your two daughters and we will get them."

My parents became alarmed and decided that my sister and I had to leave. My sister had just passed final examinations. With a high school diploma she could enter a university. I would have to switch schools. With the help of friends my parents rented a room with a Polish family in the city of Lodz, a large industrial center. We were introduced to our landlords as Christians who came from the province to study. My sister registered at the University of Lodz and I was accepted into a state high school. Only on rare occasions when we met our parents and with them visited Jewish friends did we briefly become Jews. Otherwise we were passing.

Neither my sister nor I liked this change. The anonymity of our surroundings, so indispensable to our safety, irritated me. I felt rebellious. I resented being forced once more to become someone else, but I continued to play the role; I had to. But inside me my objections multiplied. No doubt resentment with disappointment prevented adjustment. As long as I stayed in Lodz I felt like an outsider, an outsider that was aware of the ugliness of the city, the narrowmindedness of my fellow students, the uninspired instructions of my teachers, the dullness of the landlords, and my own restless loneliness.

My parents decided to leave Poland. My father found the Communist rule particularly distasteful. His independent spirit and tolerance were incompatible with their confining policies. Even more important, Poland was still unsafe for Jews. To further this end he became Mietek's business partner. This he did in addition to running two factories. In a new and strange country money could be very useful.

Our factories continued to prosper. But soon the authorities began to nationalize large business enterprises and there were rumors that this would soon apply to our chemical factory as well. The factory was too big even for partial private ownership. When transfer became a reality the workers called for a special meeting, at which they decided to press the authorities to let my father stay on as director. My father tried to dissuade them from launching a vigorous protest, but without informing them that he was not interested in the position. By 1945 people could not simply choose to leave the country and our plan to leave Poland had to remain secret. Giving up the directorship of the chemical factory was a step in the right direction; it would mean one less tie to Poland.

We had no choices. Germany was the only country not fully under Russian control that shared a border with Poland. As my parents planned our departure from Poland they were aware that if we reached parts of Germany occupied by Western powers we would not be returned to Poland.

Even with the authorities trying to protect them, Lublin was becoming less safe for my parents. In fact, there were a number of incidents that clearly showed the determination of some Poles to harm my family. Despite such danger signs, my mother and father took the time they needed to liquidate their assets.

The plan was for my father to come with my sister and me to settle us in the American Zone in Germany. After that he was to return to Poland. In his absence my mother would start winding up our affairs. After they had both finished making all the necessary arrangements they were to join us in Germany.

In 1945, on a cold wintry day my father, my sister and I sat in a car headed for the American Zone in Germany. With Mietek at the driver's seat, the other passengers were his fiancée, her sister, and another man, a friend. With seven people and luggage, the car was filled to capacity. But space was precious. So many of us were eager to leave. Clearly, safety was more important than comfort, and we were grateful for this rare opportunity.

Heavy snow had been falling for a week. As if in deference to us, it stopped when we were ready to leave.

Outside the city bounds, roads were covered with ice, forcing Mietek to drive cautiously. Still, even his gentle touch did not prevent our vehicle from disobedience. Several times we circled the road aimlessly, Mietek totally unable to guide the car. Through it all, he remained calm. At one point, as he unsuccessfully tried to regain control, the car stopped close to a ditch and stubbornly refused to move. We had to get out and push it into the road. This only added to our already existing strain. But Mietek tried to comfort us, by explaining that these hazardous conditions were not without value. The roads were deserted because of the ice. No traffic meant safety, safety from accidents and from border police.

For relief, we decided to stop at a country inn. However, none of us was in a sociable mood. Instead we were eager to move on and after a brief pause we did. We continued to drive slowly, unevenly and when night came we were guided by our car lights.

None of us spoke. I was grateful for the darkness and silence. My initial satisfaction at leaving Poland gave way to an uneasy feeling of rejection. Poland did not want me, it forced me to become someone else. My feeling of resentment was joined by regret, sadness, and a depressed tiredness. Yet, I wanted to be conscious of the actual crossing of the border. I was determined not to shut my eyes till this happened.

The announcement "This is the American Zone in Berlin" woke me up. Relieved, I realized that it had happened less painfully than I had expected. Right then, in this new and strange place that I could not see, I promised myself never again to pretend to be someone else. This promise I kept.

No country was eager to accept surviving Jews. For years many of them were forced to remain in Germany in camps for displaced persons (DP). Like most others my sister and I ended up in one of those DP camps. After a while my parents reached Germany as well.

At sixty-two my father died from sarcoidosis of the

lungs, an illness that had made him cough for years and caused so much trouble during the war. My mother and her new husband live in Israel as do my sister and her family. And I? I leave my Connecticut home often to visit them.